# OVERCOMING
# THE
# FEAR
# OF RIDING

By

Theresa J. Jordan, Ph.D., and Peter E. De Michele, M.Ed.

# OVERCOMING THE

# FEAR

## OF RIDING

By

Theresa J. Jordan, Ph.D., and Peter E. De Michele, M.Ed.

Breakthrough Publications, Inc.
310 North Highland Avenue
Ossining, New York 10562

For information address:

**Breakthrough Publications**
310 North Highland Avenue
Ossining, New York 10562

www.booksonhorses.com

Library of Congress Catalog Card Number: 96-078902

ISBN: 0-914327-54-2

03 02 01 00 99 98    0 9 8 7 6 5 4 3

Book design by Greenboam & Company, Ossining, NY
Jacket design by Tricia Tanassy

Photographs reprinted with permission from *The Chronicle of the Horse*

Printed in the United States of America

# DEDICATION

*To Stina, the Icelandic mare who showed me how to fly
without wings and without fear, and to my father,
Ernest A. Balazs, whose spirit is with us especially on those
private, twilight evenings when my horse and I think we are
riding out alone . . .*

~ T. Jordan

*To my wonderful wife, Anne, my reason for being. Sharing
life has made every day sweeter . . . thank you. To my mother and father, for putting me on a horse and working so hard
to give me every opportunity. To the McGraths for supporting
their unusual son-in-law.*

~ P. De Michele

# CONTENTS

# ACKNOWLEDGMENTS

My most personal thanks I owe to the Icelandic horses who have been and continue to be my friends as well as my teachers, for without them riding would not have become both my passion and my therapy. The desire to be, once again, astride one of my horses has been the single most important force pushing me beyond the barriers of physical pain, back into wellness, after some non-horse related injuries. I owe countless hours of joy to Stina and Irpa and, secondly, to Elska and Daga. I am grateful to Elding at Helms Hill for my first trail ride on an Icelandic horse, which initiated me into the wonderful world of small horses with great strength, great intelligence, and even greater hearts.

Many thanks to my instructors and trainers; to Anne Elwell, Dani Gehmacher, and Baddi Gudlaugsson for taking the time to get to know me well enough to know which horses would be a "match" and for their particular mixture of empathy, wisdom, and firmness as teachers. And to Mel Ford, who has taught me that I can get fire from my horses softly. I am grateful to those individuals with whom I have spent countless hours on the trail, including Rose Marie Sinnott and Lauren Kolski, as well as to those who have been helpful in many other ways, including Todd Jordan, Audrey and Rachel Baris, Jean Jacobus, and Hilton Williams and his staff. Thank you mom, Monty, and Tui for the precious gift without which an idea could not have grown into a book: the time to ride and to write. Lisa Mooney, our editor, deserves at least a blue ribbon for pulling together all the pieces and people who participated in the production of this book.

I am grateful to Albert Ellis, a world-class psychologist and thinker, for the privilege of studying with him, and to New York University for understanding and appreciating that Applied Psychology can apply to my work on the human-equine experience.

Finally, thank you, God, for horses.

~ Theresa J. Jordan
New York, 1996

I wish to thank all of the riders, coaches, and trainers who generously gave of their time, and whose insightful comments made this book possible. We would especially like to thank Bruce Davidson for taking the time to write the foreword, just days before earning a silver medal in the team three-day competition in the 1996 Summer Olympic Games in Atlanta, Georgia. We would like to thank Anne M. De Michele, M.Ed., for organizational and editorial suggestions throughout the book, and *The Chronicle of the Horse* for providing background history, performance information, and photos for the riders.

In addition, I would like to acknowledge the following University of Virginia faculty for their influence in the creation of this book: B. Ann Boyce, Ph.D.; Linda K. Bunker, Ph.D.; Bruce Gansneder, Ph.D.; Robert J. Rotella, Ph.D.; Gloria B. Solomon, Ph.D.; Claudia J. Sowa, Ph.D.; Valerie K. Wayda, Ph.D. (now with Ball State University).

~ Peter E. De Michele, M.Ed.

The publisher thanks Rhona Johnson, Cornelia Guest, Catherine Macaulay, and Cherry Hill for their editorial suggestions; Penny O'Prey and Bob Greenboam for design and production services; Tricia Tanassy, Maureen Gallatin, and Peter and Paul Calta for their work on the jacket design.

# FOREWORD

## BY BRUCE DAVIDSON

Riding, like other things is an exercise in knowing yourself. It involves being honest with yourself. People are searching for meaning in their lives.

Some people turn a certain age and they suddenly are unhappy with their work and they go to seminars, or they read, or they see professionals to help find themselves. I've never believed in that theory so much. I think it's always easier to just be honest with yourself.

If you are honest with yourself as a horseman, then you should know from quite an early age where you would be comfortable, where you would be most beneficial to the animal. If you can admit that, then you would also be successful in whatever aspect you decide to enter the horse world, hence the sport world, because horses *are* sport. Whether it be breeding, whether it be grooming, whether it be working in a tack shop, whether it be a saddler, whether it be as a jockey or an exercise person. So long as you are comfortable with where you are, you will be successful at that and be recognized *for* that.

Dad always said it doesn't matter what you do in life, just do it better than anybody else. I think that I've run into so many people who feel they have to come up with an excuse why they are no longer competing, or no longer riding, or can't go on with the competition the way they had set out. At the end of the day, to me, that person is just admitting that they didn't really ever have the nerve for it . . . and *that is to be respected.*

When you watch or see someone out jogging in the daytime, it doesn't matter what their figure is, it doesn't matter how distressed they look. I don't know *anyone* that sees somebody physically working at it that doesn't admire them for it. I think the same thing is true. If someone can say to themselves or say to whomever they need to have hear it, "I don't have the courage. I'm not comfortable going at such and such a level," then that is totally cool.

And you can say to me, "Bruce, I don't want to go preliminary. I just want to go to the training level and be comfortable doing that, and do a good job at that." I totally respect that, and will help that person in any way I can.

At the same time, when you see someone riding and struggling to do more than they are comfortable with, then that person is not truly a horseman or a horsewoman. They are not doing what is really best for the horse, and they are not in it for the reasons that would carry them through life.

They are in it temporarily. They might have one great horse that *they* know is capable of going to the top. Rather than letting someone else go on with it once they get it comfortably established; rather than admitting that, "I am not experienced enough;" they are holding back a creature that has the ability to do more and be recognized for what it could do.

It's wonderful to see people settle down and say, "I am *really* good at choosing horses. I have a very good eye and I know what is a nice horse. I'm not able to ride it myself above the preliminary level, or intermediate level, or whatever level one wants to name, but I can pick out a real good horse." And there are people who can do that that are not necessarily international riders themselves. And they can pick out a potential rider.

But I think what it comes down to is to be able to admit to *yourself* where *you are comfortable*—your own limits. Then work within your limits to be the best at that limit that you can be— to admit to just how frightened you were, and to realize that that isn't anything to be embarrassed of.

*I'm* scared to death of heights, not of jumping high, but being up on a bridge. You'd never get me to sky dive. You'd never get me to bungee jump. I don't even like to be a passenger in a plane.

What would be the point of me trying to make myself become a pilot? What would be the point of me trying to make myself become a recognized sky diver? That is not anything that I would be comfortable with. I'm not comfortable with handling certain types of animals or reptiles. And you can *admit* that. There are plenty of things people *can* do and *can* be comfortable at, and hence *can* be successful and can get themselves so involved in that they can make a very happy life existence, and a successful one for themselves. Isn't everyone struggling to be happy in life? And to be happy in life you have to first understand your limits, and understand your abilities.

If you are born too short without a length of leg that would make you able to become comfortable on the back of a horse . . . it doesn't mean you can't ride. It doesn't mean you can't take part in horses. It doesn't mean you can't love them for life and be successful with horses in life. But I would suggest that you don't try to be a top dressage rider. Or, if you are born to weigh 180 pounds, you have to admit you *can't* be a jockey.

If you also are not comfortable with speed, with jumping, with solid obstacles, with tall obstacles, or whatever, *admit it*. And then say, "But I can *still* make a horse good to a certain level, and I can really enjoy watching somebody who *is* better take it on and know that *I* found it, *I* established it, *I* started it, *I* recognized it, and *I* sent it where it went."

Probably the greatest teacher in my life was a woman called Lithia Schoffield. She was my father's second grade teacher, my brother's second grade teacher, my second grade teacher, and my younger brother's second grade teacher. But, above all, she was the *greatest* second grade teacher in the world.

She gave children the confidence it takes to help them realize where they *can* go in the academic world. She has watched many go on to be great lawyers, or doctors, or writers, or poets, or whatever. And she has enjoyed knowing that she had something to do with all of that along the way. She is as successful at what she does as any teacher could possibly be. She knew how to make an impression on a child at that stage in their learning. Isn't that what makes them able to go on to greater heights? So that's what we are talking about.

If people could just settle down and realize that there *is* a place in the horse world, in some capacity, for everyone who wants a place. If you sell horse insurance or become a livestock agent . . . I mean there are *so* many things, that the horse world benefits by everybody doing *well.*

---

# PART I

# UNDERSTANDING RISK
# CAN IMPROVE
# YOUR RIDING EXPERIENCE

## BE PUMPED UP
## INSTEAD OF FREAKED OUT

**CHAPTER 1**

# A GUIDE TO SUCCESS

## AN INTRODUCTION

*If you haven't enjoyed the day-to-day journey, then I hope you can take it with you [all your accomplishments] ... The one who has worn out his toys [physical and mental gifts] when he dies is the one who has won. Because he has used them, and enjoyed them.*

~ Bruce Davidson

This book is for everyone who wants to improve their riding. It is all about the attitudes, the styles of thinking, and the philosophies of successful riders and trainers, all of whom have recognized the importance of facing challenges and defeating fears—fears like not making the grade, of looking like a fool, of getting injured, of falling short of your expectations, or worse, of falling short of others' expectations. Such fears can often get in the way of happiness and success and can keep you from taking on new challenges or conquering old ones. Fear can limit your talent and impair your growth and improvement in the sport. It can also prevent you from rising to your greatest potential.

The information contained in these pages is all about conquering fear. It is not about therapy or about clinical disorders. Rather, this book is an educational tool for ordinary folks who want to learn how to get past some rough patches. Readers will learn that these rough spots pop up in front of every person who has ever had a dream of success.

This book can be your guide to success. It is written *by* riders *for* riders. We mesh the advice of great athletes and experts with the psychology of sport to fill these pages with the information you need to get the most out of your riding. The core philosophy presented here has helped countless people from all walks of life meet their goals.

We will show you how to make the most out of the talents you've got right now, and how to use them to get where you want to go. We will help you find *reasons to be successful, reasons to face your fears*, and show you *ways of doing it.* This book will help you identify the direction you want to take with your riding and help you get there.

The riders and coaches presented in this book have been selected because of their outstanding accomplishments in their discipline. We talked to them because we knew that each of them had climbed to the top of the mountain in their sport and faced their share of bad times along the way. These people know all about fears. But more importantly, they know how to defeat them, and we wanted you to know how they did it.

You may be surprised to find that the top riders in these pages are really normal people with great attitudes, philosophies, and tenacity. From the very bottom to the very top rung on the ladder of success, they know what it takes to face their fears each step of the way. You'll learn how these great riders and trainers coaxed, cajoled, and sometimes forced their way past fear, failure, pain, and obstacles to get to the top. They were willing to take the chances and the intelligent risks, and they were able to get past the failures.

Riding is a difficult and dangerous sport that involves taking risks every day. Every rider has experienced their share of hurt both from falls and from failures. We will show you how to use those failures to your advantage.

This book will do the most good if it inspires you to try new things and adopt the sensible philosophies and attitudes demonstrated in these pages. It may be difficult at first to exercise these new ideas, mostly because they may challenge the way you have always thought of yourself. How you think of yourself and your ability is a result of many past experiences and some strong habits that, combined, tend to color the way you look at the world. Often, your own way of thinking can get in the way, or block your road to success.

Fortunately, like any other habit, good or bad, the way you think is learned, and if you can learn it, then you can unlearn it. We want to help you unlearn any negative thinking you've developed over the years and show you how to think more positively and rationally so that you can achieve your goals, whatever they may be.

Habits are hard to change. Developing the right attitude that will help you take on new challenges and face your fears will require the same effort it takes to keep your heels down . . . practice, practice, practice. But, eventually, both do become second nature.

## CHAPTER 2

# UNDERSTANDING THAT NERVOUS FEELING

*If you are worried about falling, and about the fear of falling, you are going to fall.*

~ Jeff Teter

What is Fear? Many terms are thrown around when it comes time to discuss fear. Words like stress, anxiety, doubt, jitters, and fear are all intertwined in a mess we will just call nerves.

At one time or another, we've all had a case of the nerves. That sensation of tingles, of adrenaline being released into your blood, which we will call nervous energy, can prove quite bothersome. Often, we fear it might interfere with our ability to meet challenges or overcome obstacles.

## NERVOUS ENERGY

In truth, nervous energy is neither good nor bad in and of itself. The adrenaline, which causes this energy, is a powerful chemical that can lead to certain feelings and sensations that bother some and delight others. Nervous energy acts as a fuel for some people's fire (getting pumped), and a pail of water for others'(getting freaked). Either way, nerves are an unavoidable, natural part of any sport that involves risk. When we say risk, we mean everything from the risk of falling to the risk of letting yourself and others down.

Rodney Jenkins, Pan American individual and team silver medalist and the winningest American Grand Prix rider of all time (more than 75 wins) says that he felt the sensation of nervous energy every single time he competed in a big event.

> "I never rode an event where I was afraid once I walked into the ring, but I did have these nervous quirks where I'd always end up going to the bathroom 20 times before I rode. I can't believe anybody who says that they are not nervous before their event. To me, if you do not have anxieties before you walk in that ring, you are not trying."
>
> ~ Rodney Jenkins

Nervous energy does not mean you are pumped up, nor does it mean you are freaked out. It is simply the body's natural way of adapting to challenging and/or stressful situations where fighting or fleeing were once the only two options available. Adrenaline makes you more alert, stronger, and faster. It is up to you to decide whether to interpret that readiness in a positive or negative manner.

The 1995 Pan American Games dressage individual and team silver medalist, Leslie Webb, explains one especially memorable encounter with nervous energy.

> "I did my first exhibition at the Colorado Stock Show, in front of I don't even know how many thousands of people. I remember about ten minutes before I was getting on, my groom came up to me and she said that I was shaking in my boots. She said 'stick your hand out,' and I couldn't do it. I was shaking so badly!"
>
> ~ Leslie Webb

Nervous energy has some interesting effects on people. Veteran steeplechase jockey Jeff Teter, ranked sixth of all time in the United States, and the highest ranked jockey on the list who is still active, believes that, "Everyone gets nervous, including me."

> "The thing I find the funniest is, starting in the paddock I'll start yawning left and right. The adrenaline starts to pump into me. It can be embarrassing, the owners are there, and they'll say, "If you are that tired, are you ready to ride my horse . . ?""
>
> ~ Jeff Teter

## USING NERVES TO YOUR ADVANTAGE

The adrenaline that gives your body its nervous energy is there to help you. Learn to be comfortable with it. Say to yourself, "This is my body helping me." Don't let your nerves work against you, feeling that, "I'm so nervous I feel like I'm going to die. This means I'm not going to do well."

There is nothing to be gained from convincing yourself that you will do poorly, so try to enjoy the nerves. Even in times of danger it will comfort you to know that your body has pumped you full of some great stuff to help you out of difficult situations.

If you have an irrational attitude about nervous energy, you might convince yourself that the feeling is a sign of impending doom. It may cause you to avoid situations where you might feel nervous, and thus curtail your chances to learn, compete, and improve.

Greg Best, 1988 Olympic individual silver medalist, deals with any nervous energy that is bothering him by relabeling it in a more helpful and rational way. He says he,

> " . . . transforms negative energy into positive excitement. I begin to look forward to the 'up' feeling before a performance, and label the 'butterflies' as excitement rather than fear. I look forward to the chance to rise to another level."
>
> ~ Greg Best

Best is not the only top rider who uses adrenaline to his advantage. They have all learned that the sensation feels great. When viewed rationally, nervous energy can be a psychological and physical advantage and a real kick. Bruce Davidson, five-time Olympian and the only repeat world champion in the history of three-day eventing, says he enjoys having nerves.

"That is part of the fun of it . . . that I'm so anxious. Why else would you go on a roller coaster? Because it is a thrill for the moment."

~ Bruce Davidson

### PUMPED UP, NOT FREAKED OUT

Four-time Olympian dressage rider and trainer Robert Dover hits the nail right on the head when he explains the difference between having a rational and irrational response to nervous energy.

"[I have had nerves] a million times absolutely. There isn't a competition where a certain kind of nerves is not present. You want a certain kind. There is one kind that is constructive and one that is destructive. The good kind comes totally with experience. Those who say that they are never nervous are rare and at the end are not necessarily the victors."

~ Robert Dover, *The Chronicle of the Horse*, March 1996.

Dover is referring to the difference between being pumped up and being freaked out by a case of the nerves. Certainly some situations might cause you to feel more nervous than others, but it is still up to you to decide whether you want to be rational or irrational about it. In short, are you going to let the feeling help you or hurt you?

Most elite competitors crave the rush of adrenaline that comes before a competition because they know they need it to win. Former top professional and now top amateur steeplechase

jockey Colvin "Greg" Ryan explains that the pressure of competition gives him the nervous energy he, too, loves. Over the years
he has noticed how some others seem to crumble when facing
the same situations he so enjoys.

> "I love the pressure. I do. I mean in the big races like
> the Gold Cup [top steeplechase race], the money is on
> the line. I love it. I really love it. But, I think my record
> is probably best at the race track. It's always fun to get
> out there and see the crowd. I know people at the track
> and the pressure is really on. You can see that some
> people in the jock's room, they'll be running in the
> fourth race. They'll be sitting there doing nothing for
> three hours, waiting for the race, and some people will
> just wilt. You can see it. They are just dying . . . saying,
> 'let's just get it over with.' "
>
> ~ Greg Ryan

What Ryan has just described is a situation in which one
person thrived and used his nerves to his advantage, while others
around him allowed these same nerves to wear them down.

Experience helps us to deal with nervous energy in a productive and positive way. Maturity also plays a part in understanding nervous energy, as Dover pointed out. That is because
adrenaline is often misunderstood at first and thought of as an
uncomfortable or terrible sensation.

People often mistakenly believe that they must get rid of
their nervous energy in order to perform well. Not so. That energy is there for you to use or abuse. It is up to you to decide if
you are going to use it to your advantage.

## SIZING THINGS UP

The sizing up process is more elaborate than just the interpretation of adrenaline. It involves the way you think of yourself as a
rider, the way you think about factors in the situations you face,
and the goals you have set. You can be rational or irrational in

evaluating your own skills, and you can be rational or irrational in evaluating your environment (the horse, the trainer, the terrain, the weather). You are being irrational if you are hurting your chances of pursuing your goals. You are being rational if you are helping yourself pursue your goals.

When sizing things up, people typically rank how good they are, i.e., their ability, against the difficulty of the challenge, i.e., the risk, and then decide whether they have what it takes to surmount a challenge. For most, this is a split-second process that matches the size of the risk with the size of the ability.

Below is an example of how one rider might potentially size up a challenge.

*Situation:* A beginner rider considers jumping a fence for the first time during a lesson.

*Assessing Risk:* The rider determines how much she trusts the horse as well as the instructor's ability not to overface her (push her too far). She also considers the fence's size, its appearance, and other factors like the terrain and the weather. She might determine the difficulty of the task based on other people's success and failure at it.

*Assessing One's Own Abilities:* In determining her abilities, the rider thinks about her training and her feelings of preparation. She also thinks about how well she can perform the requisite skills that add up to a good jump—eyes up, heels down, grab some mane, and so on. Other factors she might consider include past practices and her enjoyment or dislike of the nervous energy she is feeling. She might also think about other people similar to herself who have surpassed this challenge. Were they better skilled, equally skilled, or less skilled than she? Finally, she might listen to what people around her are saying to tip the scales. Are they saying she can or cannot accomplish this thing?

*Assessing Costs vs. Benefits:* If this particular rider is motivated and jumping is an important goal for her, she will look high and low for a safe way to jump the fence despite her fears. She might decide to jump it in parts (maybe by first walking over a log and then jumping a low pole; or by changing either the horse or the setting) until she can accomplish the task. The point is, she will size up the situation, assess the risk against her own abilities, and, upon deciding that the benefits outweigh the costs, go ahead and meet the challenge.

On the other hand, if our rider had decided that jumping that fence would not help her reach her goals, she would have little motivation to do so, and it would show as the level of risk increased further down the line. For the higher the risk of injury or failure, the less likely anyone is to take on a challenge. There needs to be motivation and a goal before a rational person will assume a risk.

## BEING A HOPEFUL REALIST

People who take rational risks (either mental or physical) are called *hopeful realists*. These are people who can size things up, who have a sense of what they can and cannot control and a sense of where they are going. Every risk they take has a sensible purpose. They know the costs and the benefits.

The best riders in the world are hopefully realistic. THEY KNOW:
- Themselves and their abilities.
- How to ride within their limits and those of their horse.
- How to find smart chances.
- How to realistically and rationally assess all aspects of a challenge.

Nervous energy serves as a signal to the presence of a challenge. But, in addition to those sensations, there is a mental evaluation, or sizing up, of the risks and benefits of facing a challenge.

Cherry Hill—rider, trainer, and judge in hunt seat, western, and dressage; and author of several riding books—highlights the differences between the gut response (nervous energy) and the mental evaluation (sizing up process) when describing a personal trail riding experience.

> "My husband and I were on a rugged 'trail-less' ride in the Colorado Rockies. At one point, we came to the edge of a vertical rock wall with a precipice of over 1,000 feet. When we rode our horses to the edge to take a look, I got a flurry of butterfly activity in my gut, and when I urged my horse to walk along the edge so I could get a better view, I found my legs had turned to rubber. My horse was very calm and obedient and intellectually I knew my chances of falling over the edge were pretty slim, but the physiological sensation was there nonetheless. This was a great insight for me."
> ~ Cherry Hill

Hill saw both sides, the mental and the physical aspects. She did not put any spin on the experience, or try to interpret it in any way. It was not a kick, nor was she frightened. She simply felt a neutral feeling of nervous energy. When analyzing the situation, her assessment of the potential risk came back with a message from the brain that the situation posed very little risk.

This highly analytical sizing up process is very much a learned habit—one that requires the rider to become an analyst of both his or her personal abilities and the nature of the difficulties faced. There are many variables that enter into the equation. For example, if Hill had experienced a near miss, or an actual fall from a height in the past, or if she had once seen someone else suffer either of those, she might have learned to

---

## CHERRY HILL'S CASE

| MENTAL RESPONSES | PHYSICAL RESPONSES |
|---|---|
| 1. Curiosity in cliff. | Adrenaline surge. Body prepares for challenge. |
| 2. Examined the cliff. Saw the height and the situation. | Rubbery legs, "butterflies." Ready for any challenge. |
| 3. Sizing up. Match situation and abilities. | Adrenaline maintenance. Prepared for interpretation. |
| 4. Neutral interpretation of the feeling as unlikely challenge. | Need for activation reduced—gradual adrenaline. |

---

analyze the situation as being more dangerous and perhaps avoided it. If the task was very important to her goals as a rider, she would have to work very hard to make sure she got an honest appraisal of the real risks she faced and the real skills she possessed, and what she really needed to do to accomplish her goal.

You might ask why someone would ever voluntarily do something so dangerous. They might be highly motivated, and the thought of not doing that particular thing might conceivably stand in the way of their happiness. If they were thinking rationally about achieving their goals, they would have a clear understanding of both the risks and the strategies needed to overcome the challenges.

The notion of assigning any right or wrong to doing risky things is a highly personal one. It is more about a rider's own perspective than any objective criteria, as we will discuss later.

## CHAPTER 3

# THE NATURE OF
# A CHALLENGE

*Don't evaluate yourself and what you're doing by other people's standards or judgments.*

~ Valerie Kanavy

Among the many struggles most riders face in their training is deciding what types of challenges to tackle on the way to their dreams. At each juncture, a rider must determine which risks really are worth taking.

Risks that cause fear are those of:
- *Injury*
- *Failure.*

Great riders are conservative when it comes to risking injury, but they are bold in challenging failure. When they prepare for practices and competitions, they work to reduce the risk of injury. While all the great riders we interviewed experience a certain degree of fear over becoming injured, none found any benefit from fearing failure.

Like them, the risk of *failure* is one you, too, should take as often as possible, whereas the risk of being *injured* should be minimized. It is important, however, that both types of risk make sense to you in terms of moving you further toward your goals.

Dressage rider and trainer Carol Lavell—team bronze medalist in both the 1992 Barcelona Olympics and the 1994 World Equestrian Games—has a very straightforward approach to helping herself and her students conquer their fears. She feels risks worth taking are those that might lead to failure, not injury.

> "You learn in the competition arena, so you need to go a whole lot. You'll have the same nerves before each test. But every test will be a little better for you to ride because soon you won't be wondering about where you turn right and left. When you know the test, you'll be

*Olympic and World Equestrian Games bronze medalist Carol Lavell says that, "You learn in the competition arena, so you need to go a whole lot. You'll have the same nerves before each test. But every test will be a little better . . ."*

able to start to ride the horse. Until that happens, you cannot ride well in the ring.

"You have to keep going. It takes a long time to be able to do well in a ring [in competition]. If your horse isn't a good horse, you are going to have to deal with that too, but he's not going to be different in the competition than he is at home. We work really hard on that. Nothing ventured nothing gained . . .

"The tension and the fear of failure is the same at Grand Prix as it is at training level test one. If I have riders who have real problems with fear of failure, I start them off [going] to as many schooling shows as possible."

~ Carol Lavell

Lavell says she has "wisened up" over the years and is taking fewer risks these days, particularly those involving any risk of injury. Lavell, previously an event rider, claims that changing disciplines and altering her goals was one of the first steps she took toward finding an acceptable level of risk in her riding. Below, she discusses a challenge she walked away from after making a realistic assessment of her skills.

"I started to smarten up a little bit when I had the horse Better And Better. It was just before the Olympic Games in 1976 and I was headed for three-day [eventing]. I had never even been in more than one international competition [but she was long-listed on the U.S. team]. I wasn't a rank novice. I already had my horse going well at advanced level and he was ready to go. The only problem was that *I* wasn't ready. I knew nothing about doing that level of competition. I hadn't ridden in England and I had no experience with that kind of stuff. I wasn't prepared for that. I said, 'No way, I'm going to get killed...' I smartened right up and sold him to a really good event rider, Michael Plumb [five-time Olympian] and look what happened [they won the team gold in 1976]. Someone asked me if I wasn't just a little bit sorry to give the horse up. You know, I was very unhappy that I had to sell a horse that I had such a relationship with, but not the least bit unhappy about not riding in the Olympic games in three-day. It was a very tough, enormous course and I was nowhere near knowledgeable enough, skillful enough, or experienced enough to do that, and yet I was headed right for it."

~ Carol Lavell

Lavell went on to explain that while she found dressage also full of challenges and risks, she avoided those she thought she could not, or would rather not, handle by making arrangements with another rider.

This same attitude carries over to her coaching as well. She says that she has now changed her attitude about what constitutes acceptable and unacceptable risks for her students.

"When I'm in a clinic situation and I see a horse doing something to a rider I ask the rider, 'Has this horse done this before?' If they say, 'No. Never,' I see if we can get around this behavior. But if they say, 'Oh yes, and we tried all these different things to stop it. And she did actually fall over backwards four or five times last year . . . ,' I say, 'I'm really, very sorry, but I'm not interested in hurting a rider. I know this is your only horse and you have a lot of money invested in this horse, but you don't have to make a point to me that you are not a quitter or that you are not afraid, or that this is your horse and you must deal with it. I don't want you even thinking about making that kind of point. And I don't want you to ever think of this as failure. What I want you to think about it is that it's a matter of personal safety, and it has nothing to do with

failure. If you can't get this horse to do things that you
want it to do, let's just get on to the next, because life is
for the living, so let's go out and live it.' "

~ Carol Lavell

Lavell believes that a rider should take risks of failing
because you can live through those. And, as she notes, "The
pressure is all internal." But when it comes to taking a chance of
getting hurt . . . think very carefully.

"I tell them [students] that, 'You haven't failed here.
You acted intelligently as a human being because you
are a survivor and there are other things to do with
horses besides have a horse fall over backwards on you
and kill you.

"Some of the smart ones [students] let the physical fear
take over. But then, those who are in denial, really I'm
always in awe of them. They are foolish, they can't be
that stupid, so they must be in denial."

~ Carol Lavell

The following examples show how determined Lavell is to
keep her students safe, and they exemplify the trouble she has
convincing students that they are in unhealthy situations. Lavell
was teaching at a clinic where a student's horse was putting on
quite a display of dangerous behavior. Because she was having
trouble convincing the rider that she was in a dangerous situation, Lavell decided to have the gallery of unmounted students
who were there to help her evaluate the situation.

"With 200 people in the gallery I said, 'Gallery, let's
just vote. Does anybody here think that this girl has
provoked this behavior today?' One-hundred percent of
them said, 'No.' I said, 'Do you think that the horse is
being asked to do something unreasonable?' Again,
one-hundred percent of them said, 'No.' I said, 'Do

you think that this horse is in pain?' Well, about half
said that was a little difficult to tell, and I said, 'Yup. I
agree. It might be that something is wrong with this
horse. But that doesn't mean that we go and ride him
over and over and over again, thinking that it's going to
go away. It could be some pain and it could be something wrong, but it's going to have some really erratic
and eruptive kind of behavior that's going to hurt you.
But do we agree that this person should not ride this
horse until we figure that out?' One-hundred percent
said 'Yes.' "

~ Carol Lavell

Lavell does whatever she can to keep the sport safe, and she
does whatever she can to convince people to take the healthy
risks, too. Below, she explains about her rational way of taking
on the risk of failure, from the lower to the more advanced levels
of dressage competitions.

"The other fear that really everyone has is fear of failure. I have a talk that I give that starts with . . . trying to
ride in dressage is really difficult because there is so
much fear of failure, and so much fear that everyone is
watching you and you are going to make lots of mistakes in the ring. The best medicine, of course, is to go
to the ring and look at everybody else making mistakes.
Then you feel a whole lot better. If they can do it, you
can do it just as badly.

"In the beginning, you're out there riding at training
level test one and your test is probably at 7:30 in the
morning. You're out there white-knuckled with fear
because the judge will see you making mistakes, and
because you are afraid of what all those people will
think of you. But, if you look around really carefully,
there are two people sharing a bag of doughnuts and

coffee, and one person sitting in a chair reading a news-
paper. The other three people are waiting for the next
horse to come. So actually no one is looking at you and
no one cares . . . just you and your groom. Then you get
up the line a little and you get some of those wonderful
pictures back from dressage at Devon (Pennsylvania).
Here you are at your Prix St. Georges test. You've
worked so hard to get your horse there and now you're
really able to ride better in the ring, even though you
think thousands of eyes are on you. So, there you are
afterward, with some beautiful picture that some pho-
tographer took of you trotting extended trot across that
arena at Devon. In the grandstands behind you in the
picture there are maybe four people behind you. Two
are talking to each other, one's looking the other way,
and one's reading the program . . . and, yeah . . . yeah,
they are really staring at you waiting for you to make a
mistake . . . Oh the pressure!

"The pressure is all internal. Now, there are people who
do come out to watch the very good riders, and that's a
bit more pressure. There were about 13,000 people
who watched me do my freestyle last year at Devon,
and that's a lot of pressure. I deal with that kind of fear
of failure by thinking and saying to myself that lots of
people wished they were right where I am. They want
to be up here doing this too. Yup, they want to do it.
They are all riding with you and having a good time.
And, a lot of people don't have the slightest clue about
what you are doing. When you make a mistake maybe
no more than fifty percent of them can tell.

"Then there are some very good people out there who
will be looking at you. They will notice when you make
mistakes. But, if you are very good about going to the
ring, you can watch them ride and see them make the

same mistakes. Yeah, there are a few more people watching now, but they're making mistakes just like you.

"You know there's the little saying about improving: 'every day in every way I'm getting better and better.' That's how I named my event horse and that's the way I feel about riding. You can't learn except on the playing field. Then you get all the way to the Olympic Games and . . . you're nightmare has come true. The people watching you are experts and they are waiting for you to make mistakes, and they are looking at you . . . true, true, and true. And you know how I deal with it? You say, 'You know, I wouldn't be here if I weren't one of the best,' and, 'I earned the right to be on this playing field with the world's best.' I mean, how did I get here . . . walk?

"I earned the right to be here and I'm riding with the best and the reason I'm riding with the best is because I am one of the best. The only thing different about the Olympic Games and riding way back at Devon and some of those other competitions . . . is the prize. But the tension and the fear of failure is the same right up at Grand Prix as it is at training level test one."

~ Carol Lavell

Jeff Teter says that he had a hard time with the whole idea of fear. He said that he really did not have fear of injury or failing on his mind. He said that if the injury aspect of fear ever became a factor in his mind, he would reconsider riding.

" . . . at least from my position anyway, as soon as fear comes into it I'm going to retire. It's hard when you come across things that are fearful because, you know, people like me and everybody else you talk to don't look at it as fear. I mean you *can't* look at it like that. To me, fear is when you are afraid, and if you're afraid you

would not be riding. I don't think you'll find many
[riders] who are going to use the word fear. They're
going to maybe use . . . I don't know, maybe, have an
anxious moment."

~ Jeff Teter

As for letting people down, or failing to make it to the winners circle, Teter says that those things,

" . . . never really entered my mind. Because to me,
there are enough other things to worry about without
worrying about what other people are thinking or worrying about whether I'm going to mess up."

~ Jeff Teter

Teter explains that the best way around all of those fears is
in the preparation. He begins that process before the season, and
continues a carefully organized routine for every race. He plans
what he needs to do to win, and what he needs to do to be safe.
That is why he fears neither injury nor failure—not because
there is zero possibility of injury or failure, but because he does
as much work as he can to minimize the possibility.

"The biggest thing is preparation. My thing is preparation long before I even get a leg up in the saddle on the
day of the race. You need to get fit, so I run and condi-
tion myself to be as fit as I can possibly be. And then,
the Monday of the week before the races you look at
the entries, see what you're riding, see what your oppo-
sition is and figure out the preparation. I figure how
the race is going to set up from the time you get down
to the start, throughout the race. My mind is on those
things all week.

"I think the preparation cuts down all the problems
that can happen. The preparation is the biggest thing.
You can try to cut down on all the probable mistakes

and scenarios that you don't want to happen.

"Then, from the time I get on the horse, you know, I've sort of picked out three or four horses that I think are the horses to beat. I think that these are essential things that need to be done long before the starter drops the flag.

"There's a tremendous amount more effort and work involved in getting into that winners circle than I think most people really realize."

~ Jeff Teter

One source of fear is listening to what others say you should do, and comparing yourself to how you match up to what *they say* is perfection. The happiest people in life are the ones who are *doing what they want to do* and overcoming challenges, fear, and rough patches in the thing they love. They measure success by their own improvement on their way, not by comparison to other peoples' standards. Bruce Davidson says this about comparisons:

"I've had people compare me to others. I haven't compared myself to anyone else. How can I, since I'm not done [with who I am] yet?"

~ Bruce Davidson

Valerie Kanavy, gold medalist in the World Endurance Riding Championships at the 1994 World Equestrian Games, says that comparing yourself to outside standards is what creates fear of failure.

"Fear of failure has first of all to do with, I guess, the goals you set. Just because you may not win an event, a race, or come out with the blue ribbon, [it] is not a failure. If you are learning and growing and doing all the time, the fact that you've given a good performance, or that you've done a really good job, is a win. Don't evaluate yourself and what you're doing by other peoples' standards or judgments."

~ Valerie Kanavy

Davidson says, "I've had plenty of students, and I've tried to help them understand that they are *not trying to beat anybody else*. Just take care of yourself and your horse and do a better deal than you've ever done before, and the results will come."

## CHAPTER 4

# GOOD RISKS vs BAD RISKS

## FACING FEAR

## AS A MATTER OF PERSONAL GOALS

*It's what you do with your chance when you get it, as to whether you get to be successful.*

~ Jeff Teter

When people stand at the edge of their own abilities in riding, when they are trying to get even better than they already are, the challenges can become very large, some of them questionable, some of them even dangerous. At this point the difference between a good and a bad risk is often based upon personal needs, desires, and goals. In trying to attain those goals, riders can often experience feelings of fear over failure or over getting hurt. Both require an assessment of the costs and benefits involved. In this chapter, we will help you sort out those fears, and show you how they can fit into your own personal desires and goals by showing you some examples of how top riders have fit challenges into their own philosophies and yours.

In the end, your goals and dreams in riding will ultimately determine what kinds of risks you will choose. Your direction in the sport will play an enormous part in every decision you make, every challenge you avoid, and every challenge you face. For now, understand that the difference between good and bad challenges is not always so obvious.

The best riders know themselves very well and are realistic about both their abilities and about the rigors of the risks and challenges they face. They have a sense of hopeful realism, which enables them to minimize the danger of injury and failure while maximizing their success.

After reading the next several pages, you may find that some of the challenges our riders took in order to obtain their goals blur the line between acceptable and unacceptable risks. The elusive nature of the line comes from the fact that rationality is in the eye of the beholder. It is built on personal goals and personal motives.

To give you a better feel for where this hazy line is, and how it is drawn, we present several examples of how different top-notch riders have drawn personal boundaries to separate those challenges they consider good risks from those challenges they consider to be bad risks. Every example may not apply to every reader. Examine the sections that you can relate to and use them to help you set your own personal boundaries and limits for each risk.

## BRUCE DAVIDSON

### GOOD RISKS

Bruce Davidson describes two situations in which his motivation, goals, and a sense of reality guided his decisions to take on challenges. Davidson has an extraordinary philosophy on both the sport and life, and that is reflected in the way he pursues them both.

The setting for this first situation was the 1988 Olympic Trials. During the trials Davidson crashed on one of his less experienced horses, breaking two ribs. Nonetheless, he went on to ride his other two mounts, producing the two fastest cross-

*Bruce Davidson considered broken ribs a good risk when he qualified for the 1988 Olympic team.*

country rounds of the day and securing a spot on the team. For him, deciding to continue competing with the other horses constituted a good risk.

> "I had four horses that day at the trials. The first two were highly inexperienced, and the last two were the most experienced. When I fell [on the second ride] I knew it hurt like hell, but it was not life-threatening. I had not punctured a lung, and all I had to do was not fall again. I was going from getting on the greenest to the two most experienced. I knew them [the horses], and they knew me, and I knew the course. I knew I could get the job done under adverse circumstances."

"It was not life-threatening. It was just painful, and it was my choice and nobody made me. In fact, many people tried to talk me out of it. I can choose what I can do and what I cannot do."

~ Bruce Davidson

## BAD RISKS

Davidson is very aware of his own abilities and of the situations he faces. Part of that understanding entails knowing when not to go ahead with a challenge. It is knowing when you simply cannot safely go through with something, for one reason or another.

"I broke my collar bone at Kentucky this year and I could not use my right hand . . . I could not go on . . . I said that this was the end of my day. Nobody can tell you really what kind of pain you are in."

~ Bruce Davidson

## DAVIDSON'S PHILOSOPHY ON RIDING

When Bruce Davidson wants something, he is motivated to pursue it, and he is willing to work through adversity to reach his goals. He pointed to this distinction quite powerfully when he explained that he's "allergic to pain." He also explained that it was not difficult to make the decision to keep going despite pain at the '88 Olympic trials when he was injured.

"If painting houses is what I loved and I was injured in the same way [broken ribs], I would say that I'd paint the lower half this month [because he couldn't lift his arm] and the upper half next month when my arm heals. If I were working a job I didn't like I'd call in sick and say that the doctor said that I should take six weeks off until it heals."

~ Bruce Davidson

Davidson explained that he has little reason to fear failing. Some people might say that his low concern with failure may be due to the fact that he is so successful. That is like putting the cart before the horse. His low concern for failure and his philosophy of life and sport allowed him to become so successful. His low concern with failure stems from his wonderful philosophy in riding, and that makes him more likely to succeed. It is little wonder that he has dominated the sport for so many years. He does what he does for all the right reasons.

"I'm not an award-oriented person. I don't ride to amaze or for the records. I ride because of my connection to the horse. There was never any question that I would get what I wanted from riding. I get that every day. If I were a psychiatrist, or any kind of other professional too, I'd be involved in the work for myself and what it could do for others.

"If somebody has fear, then they are in it for the short term anyway. They haven't looked at themselves deeply enough to find that they are not comfortable where they are. They may need to back up and stop trying to be recognized by blue ribbons and silver plates and enjoy what the whole thing is about. Maybe stop taking riding lessons, and start taking training horse lessons.

"It is the day-to-day process and the day-to-day journey. If you haven't enjoyed the day-to-day journey, then I hope you can take it with you [all your accomplishments] . . . The one who has worn out his toys [physical and mental gifts] when he dies is the one that has won. Because he has used them, and enjoyed them.

"I think that people who have fear of failing haven't looked deeply enough into the stages of life. They are saying, 'If it does not work for me, if you put two years into this and it doesn't work . . . then what next?' If I don't get my results, it does not mean I'm going to can it. I was always in it for the day-to-day.

"If I were a record-oriented person I probably would have gone about it all [my career] very differently, and I certainly would seek the press. It is not fame or fortune I seek. I do it for my connection with the animal and my enjoyment of working with them as a species. The results are my way of confirming that connection, that I am getting the message across."

~ Bruce Davidson

## LESLIE WEBB

**GOOD RISKS**

Leslie Webb explains how she has taken on some challenging horses she felt she could change, feeling that, in terms of her career, these constituted good risks.

"I've taken on some very difficult horses that I really felt I could change around. I knew it would have taken at least six months . . . But I felt ready because I definitely had some excellent training. I spent ten years working with Erich Bubell my coach. He gave me excellent coaching . . . so, every time I got on I followed his guidelines. I already had a blueprint as to what I needed to do for each scenario . . . and I never ran into a scenario that I eventually could not win. Yes, I was very nervous, but I was never nervous enough to not get on."

~ Leslie Webb

*Pan American Games individual and team silver medalist Leslie Webb says that she never cared what people thought of her riding. "Measure the success not by the score but by how you feel about it. Too many people are so concerned about the ribbons."*

Webb is also very forward about taking on other risks, even those that could lead to failure. Although she admits to feeling nervous, she still takes the chances. She has experienced what she calls "pre-performance jitters" in the past and has faced them by continuing to compete and by developing mental routines to practice before the competition (see Chapter 8).

### BAD RISKS

Webb also has a firm idea of how much risk she is willing to take when the result is personal injury.

"If a horse comes to me and he's horrible and tends to rear and do horrible, horrible things, I assess the problem. Is he 16 hands, or is he 17.2? I have sent horses home that were beyond my limit. I just knew that I could not deal with it, and that's being smart."

~ Leslie Webb

## WEBB'S PHILOSOPHY OF RIDING

Webb has some basic personal guidelines that she uses in making decisions about taking on challenges which revolve around her solid philosophy on riding.

"I have never really cared what other people thought about the way I rode. I'm either going to go out there and make a fool of myself, or I'm going to go out there and win a class, but I have never really cared what other people said about my riding. And the reason [is] that nine times out of ten, the person on the sidelines who is cutting you down the most is the person who can't even post the trot. I've always stuck that in the back of my mind.

"I try to tell my students that too. The other thing I tell them is, when a judge judges you, [she] does not know what your problems are and has not seen the progress from two months ago to today, or has not seen the progress from three months ago to today. If you have a little bit of a mistake and she marks you down, at least you and I know that it was ten times better than it was two months ago.

"Measure the success not by the score but by how you feel about it. Too many people are so concerned about the ribbons."

~ Leslie Webb

Webb's philosophy also extends to the type of challenges she will accept.

"I've been in the situation where I fear injury. I think that each person . . . needs to know their boundaries, and their limitations."

~ Leslie Webb

## MARTHA JOSEY

**GOOD RISKS**

Barrel racing champion and teacher Martha Josey—team gold and individual bronze medalist from the 1988 Calgary Olympics, and the only barrel racer ever to compete in the Nationals for four different decades—discusses the two injuries she sustained earlier in her career and how she still considers them to have been good risks. She was motivated by her love of the sport and of competing and kept going, despite adversity.

"In 1968, the first year that I joined the Professional Rodeo Association, my horse was running out of the arena and he hit a hard area, did a flip in the air, came down, and I had a concussion. I still decided to ride after it. The doctors didn't think that I would ride for months . . . and I rode about six days later.

"I've had several horse-related accidents. In 1982 I was doing a video training tape and using a young horse. He started jumping and lunging and bucking. I broke my pelvis in three places and I broke my arm, and everything. They said that it was possible I could never ride again. Well, at first they said I might never walk again, and then they said I'd never ride again. That was in June and I won my first barrel race in September."

~ Martha Josey

*Olympic medalist and barrel-racing great Martha Josey says that common sense is the key to safe riding. "I get such joy out of riding."*

## BAD RISKS

In contrast, she explains that there was one risk she never considered worth taking since there was no benefit to it, nor would it help her pursue her goals.

> "I would be scared and get off a horse if I thought it would be way too much for me. I've got the common sense to say no that this is too much horse. You need to use lots of common sense around horses."
>
> ~ Martha Josey

Josey knows what she can and cannot realistically do. She rode with some injuries because she knew she could. She was motivated by a goal, by the desire to keep doing something that she loved, and to compete. But she wouldn't ever ride a horse she did not think she could handle.

## JOSEY'S PHILOSOPHY OF RIDING

Josey loves what she does and thinks it keeps [her] young. She enjoys all aspects of the business, saying,

> "I'd just be devastated without them [horses], probably because I get such a joy out of riding, and training and teaching. It's such a healthy sport, and I think if you use lots of common sense around horses [you will be safer]."
>
> ~ Martha Josey

## JEFF TETER

### GOOD RISKS

Steeplechase jockey Jeff Teter says, "I think the biggest thing is to know your limitations." After 14 years of experience he is being honest and realistic when he adds that, "I feel I have very few or no limitations when it comes to a hard horse."

Teter is a conservative rider. Most of the risks he takes are based on each horse's ability. He prepares well and knows each animal's capabilities. He also does not seek out problem horses or situations.

> "With a green horse, maybe he had a good experience in the last race. He didn't try any tricks. Maybe I can get down on the rail a little, and save a little more ground here and get a little closer to the inside. Or maybe you do that once and you see that he's thinking about try-ing to duck, and so you think, whoa maybe that's not a good idea just yet.

"I think all the successful people try to minimize the
risks as much as possible. The fewer risks I have to take,
the less chance something negative is going to happen,
or the less chance I'm going to get hurt. I think that all
successful people in our field . . . that's what [they] do.
The real work is in the preparation. You know, if you
do all your homework beforehand, you cut all the risk
factors down tremendously, and, hopefully you take the
chance of getting hurt out of play."

~ Jeff Teter

## BAD RISKS

Teter explains that there are certain limits to what horse he will
ride, and what things he will try in a race. He uses caution for
his sake, and for the horse's learning experience.

"I don't go out of my way to get a horse that could be a
problem. I've been doing this long enough. Why take
the risk of getting on something dangerous? When I
first started, I got on anything. But, I can say over the
past two to three years I haven't gone out of my way to
get rides."

~ Jeff Teter

When Teter races green horses, he seeks the good experience
for himself and the horse first, the victory second. He explains
what he considers bad risks when seeking these experiences.

"I try to get that horse to have as good an experience as
possible. If he can win within himself, fine, he'll win.
But you don't go out of your way to save ground, cut
corners, to put him in a bad position for the sake of
winning the first time. Don't get him pinned down on
the inside and really give him a chance to duck out at
the wing. I think the biggest thing is that you try to
not get yourself in a position to create a problem.

*Three-time National Steeplechase Association Rider of the Year Jeff Teter says that, "the real work is in the preparation . . . if you do all the homework beforehand, you cut all the risk factors down tremendously."*

"You need to ride within that horse, whether he's a first time starter, a seasoned campaigner, or whether he's in between. You need to ride according to the amount of experience the horse has.

"With a first-time starter your main goal is not necessarily winning. You can be head to head for the lead coming down to that last fence, but I'm still not going to drop his head and go for the big one and go flat out over these fences. My main goal would be to get to the other side of that fence with its four legs underneath, and then drive for the wire.

"That is different from what somebody with a little less experience might do. They are in the heat of the moment and say, 'Oh, here I've got a chance to win and go flat out to the board and drive him to the ground,' because of inexperience. They go for the heat of the moment rather than what was best for the horse in the situation.

"I'm not going to have a horse wound out 100% to his capacity. I'm not going as hard and as fast as he can to that last fence. I'm always going to save a little bit in hand. [My] goal is to get them across the finish line with me on top of them and them underneath me rather than going flat out, hell bent for election to that last fence, just to win. They'll go down in a heap at that last fence. Maybe two or three times out of ten, you'll get away with it, and you may win . . . but I think that chances are that seven out of the ten times, something bad is going to happen. He may not fall, but he may miss the fence, and you give up two or three lengths, whereas if you had just tried to get over it and then pushed after that you maybe wouldn't have lost that ground and you still would have won anyhow.

"It takes anywhere from three to six, eight months to make [train] these horses . . . just to put yourself in a major risk position, for the sake of winning, and screwing up the good work and giving the horse a bad experience."

~ Jeff Teter

## TETER'S PHILOSOPHY OF RIDING

Teter explains that by being prepared, reducing risks, and planning carefully, most people with enough motivation and dedication could make a mark in the sport. Part of being prepared is making sure to take only the good chances and make the best use of them, including ones you might fail at.

"If you are in the game long enough and are willing to work at it, I think everybody has a fair chance. It's what you do with your chance when you get it, as to whether you get to be successful or you don't. I've seen a lot of young riders come up through the ranks . . . and it seems like...they've all been given a shot. It's just what the riders do when they are given that chance, whether they've prepared. I mean, the big thing is the ground-work. Have they done their homework? The preparatory work?  So, when you're given that kind of chance, what are you going to do with it?"

~ Jeff Teter

## RODNEY JENKINS

**GOOD RISKS**

Rodney Jenkins, retired from his show jumping career of 35 years, is now a successful steeplechase trainer in Montpelier, Virginia. Reflecting back on the methods he has used to sort out risks (both mental and physical), Jenkins says that he too has developed his own criteria for determining acceptable and unacceptable risks. He knows what kind of chances are worthwhile for him and best for his goals. He maintains a conservative view of his ability and that of his horses, and is careful to ride within both those constraints.

"You always take chances to win. When I was riding grand prix I would always look for that turn that nobody else would try. And a lot of times I got killed, but the times I made it, I won. And those times I was a hero. The other times, I was a stupid idiot to the outside world.

"I always knew that I was trying something that no one else would try. I always used turns to win. That was my philosophy. For me, I always had to find that turn to be able to win because I knew that I wasn't the kind of rider that just went hell-bent for election."

~ Rodney Jenkins

## BAD RISKS

Jenkins points out some of the things he did not do in competition because he considered them bad risks.

"I wasn't a rider who would run fast. I always rode collected in-hand, where a horse didn't make mistakes because they were off-balance and running. I never tried to ride what somebody else did. My philosophy was that you do the best you are capable of doing. If on that day that is good enough, fine. I didn't try to beat who won. I always rode within what I could do. If I knew the horse couldn't do anymore, I didn't ask him to do anymore, because I'd rather be second or third than nothing."

~ Rodney Jenkins

## JENKINS'S PHILOSOPHY OF RIDING

Jenkins's philosophy has helped him choose the kinds of risks he would take on.

"Some days I knew that maybe that winner couldn't be beaten without doing something really outrageous and stupid. But I also knew that if I tried that outrageous and stupid chance, I'd probably get nothing. You don't want to be some idiot out there trying to get killed and ruining everything that you made. Perhaps you were second today, but you didn't lose the two or three years you put in. A lot of times...you know winning is won-

*Pan American Games team and individual silver medalist Rodney Jenkins has won more grand prix competitions than any other rider in the United States. He explains that, "You always take chances to win."*

derful . . . but sometimes it just ain't your day. You still try to find a way to get some piece of the action."
~ Rodney Jenkins

Jenkins also points out that he really had very few qualms about taking chances with regard to his career, especially in the beginning. Back then, he had nothing to lose. That kind of freedom from fear gave him the ability to take chances in order to be great. Most of the things that bothered him were the business side of things, and his philosophy was to ride through those.

"It was never fear of the horse, it was the fear of where to find the next horse. For me the people who are successful year in and year out are really the horsemen who can pick the horse that can do what you're trying to do with them, whatever event it is . . . grand prix jumping, steeplechasing, racing, anything.

"The greatest fear I guess that I ever had was whether I would ever have the next great horse. I was always lucky though. I learned a lot from my father about picking horses. I always seemed to have three or four young horses ready so that when the old guys played out, the new ones fit in.

"I never owned the horse myself. I always rode for other people, and you know how you can go through a dry period. Instead of winning you are third, fourth, fifth, sixth. Well that horse, if he has won two or three or four grand prix and all of a sudden he's third or fourth for four or five weeks in a row . . . You are always waiting for that phone call, 'Well, you know he was winning. What's going on?'

"You know that fear always rose in my mind, of losing the horse, just because you had something stupid go wrong. Some variable that went wrong in the class and so forth. But I just rode through it most of the time. I never rode an event where I was afraid once I walked into the ring. I took care of that by trying to just continually show all the time, show a lot and get in the ring a lot. More chances to win, more horses to ride, and more people to work with. The business in and of itself was frightful enough. The horse part of it was the easy part of it.

"The class was always the good stuff. That's the end result of your work. The only fear you ever have is if you have, like I've had, a string of going ten grand prix placing very low . . . and you wonder if you're going to get out of that rut. But then again, preparation and changing something always overcame that."

~ Rodney Jenkins

## VALERIE KANAVY

**GOOD RISKS**

Valerie Kanavy says that there is often a balance based on her goals that dictate which risks of failure and injury she is willing to take, both for herself and for her horse. We asked her whether she would pursue the horses that were leading the pack at the beginning of a race, even if she thought their pace was too quick for that course. We wanted to know if pursuing them was a realistically hopeful risk, or if it was an inappropriate one.

> "Well, yes, you go after them if you have some real intentions of winning. Horses are getting good [fast] enough that the probability of one of those, or two of those horses in that group being able to hang on through the whole race is probably reasonable. The majority of them, half of them or more, will hit the wall and flame out."
>
> ~ Valerie Kanavy

Like Rodney Jenkins, who always looked for the quick turn for his smart risk, Kanavy is also always looking for the competitive opportunity. She explains how she would bide her time in races where the pace was too fast.

> "I've had people come up to me when I've been in races and came in second or third and say, 'I know what you were doing, you were riding right there and if they

screwed up, you had them. You never know what's going to happen.' "

~ Valerie Kanavy

Kanavy also explains how she enjoys a horse who is a little bit of a challenge, but a good risk as well.

"I do enjoy somewhat of a challenge, just because it tests your own skills. Not a dangerous horse. Actually, maybe a horse you have to finesse a little bit."

~ Valerie Kanavy

## BAD RISKS

Kanavy shares some thoughts about competition risks, and which ones seemed unacceptable to her.

"It is not so smart always going 90 miles per hour in the beginning and hoping your horse is going to be able to hang on through the end. There are people who ride that way continually. They'll be either way up or they will be out, and often they don't have a horse. You know the longevity is pretty short."

~ Valerie Kanavy

Kanavy does not mind taking on a challenging horse, but will not tolerate a dangerous one, fearing the risk.

"I've only had three dangerous ones that really stood out in my mind. They were dead bolt runaways and you never knew what would set them off. There is no communication. There is nothing. They will run themselves into a tree. It was as if they are not even interested in their own preservation. It's like the whole mind goes dead. I tried to work with them. Now I may give them one or two chances, and then that's it, they are gone."

~ Valerie Kanavy

*World Equestrian Games silver medalist Valerie Kanavy explains that you need to judge every chance you take. "Did I make my horse better, or did I make it worse?"*

## KANAVY'S PHILOSOPHY OF RIDING

Kanavy goes on to explain that part of her philosophy on taking risks involves taking into account her progress toward larger goals. She considers the following criteria when deciding if she is taking a bad risk.

> "You still have to be reasonable. You have to think that there's only so much you can do. If somebody has got a better horse on a day, then that's it. Sometimes it isn't

your day. Also, sometimes to win, you'll have to take your horse to a place where, at least for me, it doesn't make my winning sweet. You know I've won some races and had my horse pretty close to the wall, but I didn't feel very good about myself.

"You have to ask yourself after each go, did I make my horse better, or did I make it worse? It's continually building or maintaining. I'd like to think of it as continually building. But there's a gray area in our sport . . . "

~ Valerie Kanavy

Kanavy says that in matters of physical danger, she has a sense of what risks to avoid. With time and maturity, she has built a strong philosophy on safety. She knows what chances she will not take because they do not fit in with her goals. Kanavy was very honest with herself about her own abilities to handle problem horses. She stayed within the bounds of her abilities, and her goals.

"I had a pretty brave outlook in the beginning. I just sort of wanted the challenge a little bit along the way. But as I have matured there have been horses that I have gotten rid of. I've said, 'Nope, I'm not dealing with this, I don't need this. This is somebody else's problem. It's going away.' And that hasn't happened real often.

"I call it realistic assessment. I had to get to that point [it took time]. I think we all . . . have a love affair with the horse, with Black Beauty images. I hear, 'Oh, this horse was abused, he was misused.' I imagine 95 percent of the time, probably 98 percent, that statement is absolutely just false. They don't have a clue. You have to [make] realistic evaluations in terms of: Is he dangerous? Is he going to take you to where you need to go?

You can get hurt, and you can get killed . . . and *any injury takes you out of the direction you want to be going.*"

~ Valerie Kanavy

## CHAPTER 5

# COLVIN "GREG" RYAN:
# A MODEL OF A GOOD RISK

*When you realize the down side [of riding], that it is a very dangerous sport, you still do it, but you are not looking through rose-colored glasses. That's when I guess you become the veteran rider. You have to take care of your stock.*

~ Greg Ryan

Greg Ryan, a former top professional and now top amateur steeplechase jockey, explains the difference between a bad risk versus the kind of risk he considers good.

"I've seen plenty of riders going down to fences three away from home [a long way from the finish] and hitting and whipping [their horse]. That's kind of stupid. Sure, they may win a race. They may win a *single* race because I was a little more conservative three away from home. I won't win. But I'll tell you one thing. Throughout the career, I'll end up winning more races and my horse will race more often.

"Now at the last fence, if I'm in a battle and I have to roll the dice and let it go, if he [the horse] falls then that's part of the risk. But damn if he's going to fall

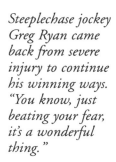

*Steeplechase jockey Greg Ryan came back from severe injury to continue his winning ways. "You know, just beating your fear, it's a wonderful thing."*

when he's not running his race in fourth place or third place, when it doesn't mean anything."

~ Greg Ryan

Ryan is no stranger to injuries. He came back to racing after a bad fall in a steeplechase race left him nearly paralyzed with a broken back. He felt that making a prompt return to riding was "Just something I had to do." Others who don't share his same goals and
motivation might claim that his return to the saddle so soon after such a serious injury was an irrational risk and hardly worth combating the fear. Below, Ryan discusses his long road back to recovery.

"I always think about [the fall and the injury]. I think

that one of my most nervous times was my first ride back. The first time was at Red Bank [New Jersey] and I think that was about five months after surgery. I just rode Circuit Bar. I wasn't going to ride, except I had ridden him seven times before. I was going to ride again . . . because I had to find out [if I could]. I didn't know how much I was going to enjoy it.

"After the accident, I remember just walking along at my mother's for the first time. I was just trying to walk and feeling so fragile just walking, just out of breath. It was a serious nine-hour operation. But, it took a long time and I was walking with my brace on, and I was wondering if I'd ever have the nerve to go galloping down to a hurdle fence ever again. I wasn't so sure.

"This was one month after surgery when you are very protective of yourself. You're in pain. I really didn't know how it would turn out. But as time went on, first I could walk, and then I started swimming. Then I went for long walks and . . . hiking in the mountains. I couldn't run yet. But, I started getting my strength back.

"As you get your strength and your fitness back you start to get your confidence back. Then I started riding. And then I schooled Circuit Bar. Nobody knew about it. In fact when I went up there to ride [at Red Bank], Jonathan Smart was named on the horse because I didn't want to go through five days of, 'Greg why are you doing this?' I really couldn't justify it. It really didn't make any sense. I remember going up there and I got the go ahead from the owners to let me ride the horse.

"I got tired and we finished second. Two weeks later I won at Montpelier. It was like a dream come true."

~ Greg Ryan

Ryan adds that his experience has given him an even greater enjoyment of racing. Just facing and conquering the challenge made him feel great, and should be a lesson to all riders who want a good excuse to conquer the fears that stand in their way. It will make you feel great.

> "You overcome it [fear] and you just go on with it. You just acknowledge it. You know, just beating your fear, it's a wonderful thing. At the end of the day in the jock's room, and everybody is [saying] 'whoa, we made it through another one.' At first you're bitching about, 'God, I didn't win the race today.' But hey, you're there in the jock's room. You're putting on your street clothes, and you are not riding in an ambulance. And it's a great feeling. And it is the same way in dressage . . . at the end of the day, there are certain things that don't show up on the balance sheet and it's never going to show up on a record book of having won. But it's a great satisfaction. You are in a dressage ring and you finish seventh, but you overcame your fear. Now that's a high! You challenged it and you overcame it. You feel good, and that's a wonderful thing.
>
> "The way I look at it, I do this for fun. I don't make my livelihood out of it. I do it for fun, and when the fear outweighs the fun for me, I'm not going to do it anymore."
>
> ~ Greg Ryan

Top riders like Ryan have an excellent understanding of their real abilities and the real challenges they face. That makes them safer and happier riders because they know the difference between reckless, irrational risks and smart, rational ones. They know how far they should try to stretch themselves because they are hopeful realists, and because they know themselves well.

### FINDING MAXIMUM ENJOYMENT WITH MINIMUM RISK

Our experts, all at the top of their profession, demonstrate quite clearly the different levels of acceptable and unacceptable risk, and the different levels of fear of injury or failure. As you can see, the differences are highly personal. There is no gold standard by which to compare yourself. However, by studying these successful individuals our hope is that you will see them as ordinary human beings with incredible aspirations. They are all people who, through trial and error, have all found a point of maximal enjoyment and minimal risk that suits them and suits their philosophy.

Generally speaking, smart risks are those that are less likely to detract from your own personal goals (like an injury), and more likely to increase your motivation (by achieving success). *It is a matter of costs vs. benefits.*

As Greg Ryan says in our case study, it is literally like the costs and benefits of finance. "It's risk management," he said. "You have to protect your stock."

You should be struck by how conservative and sensible all of these riders are. Not one of them is a daredevil. They are all great athletes and they take risks all the time, but they take risks that are smart for them because they know their weaknesses, how tough the challenge is, and they know what their goals are in the sport. They have found that maturity, in some combination of age and experience, makes for a clearer understanding of abilities, and the requirements of the task at hand.

Good, or rational risks may contribute to your fear, but if they are based on your goals and your capabilities, they can be tremendous opportunities, if chosen carefully.

Bad, or irrational risks can also engender fear, but often prove dangerous because they are made without thought, motivation, or direction. Sometimes you have to choose safety and learning and winning tomorrow over unreasonable risks and winning today.

# PART II

---

# DEVELOPING

# YOUR OWN

# SUCCESSFUL APPROACH

## APPLICATION OF
## A THEORY THAT WORKS

# THE BASICS OF
# REBT

During the early 1960s, a psychologist named Albert Ellis began to publish his theories and empirical evidence, providing the foundation for a philosophy of rational living that has evolved into Rational Emotive Behavior Therapy. Reacting against the rigid behaviorism that prevailed in American psychology at that time, Albert Ellis took exception to behaviorism's focus on changing environmental contingencies in order to change behavior. He also reacted against purely cognitive psychology designed solely to alter thoughts. He contended that the most crucial aspect of human functioning had been left out of these approaches: The interface between thoughts and both emotions and behavior.

Albert Ellis developed Rational Emotive principles to reflect his position, which finds its origins in the first century A.D. writings of Epictetus, that thoughts create feelings. The starting point of REBT was the notion, paraphrased from Epictetus, that people are not distressed by "things" or "events" but by the thoughts they have about them.

Which kinds of thoughts create distress? Thoughts that make impossible, absolute demands on oneself, others, and the world in general. Thoughts that reflect an untrue view of things. And thoughts that literally command things to be different from how they are. Ellis offers three general frameworks for irrational thoughts, *the endings of which may be filled in many ways.*

*1. I must give a perfect performance, be completely safe and without pain, feel no emotional discomfort whatsoever, etc.*

*2. You must approve of my performance completely, never criticize my behavior, give me unconditional love and support, etc.*

*3. The world must make life safe for me, treat me fairly at all times, let me achieve what I want easily and without discomfort, etc.*

*Thoughts that contain the concept of "must" (including should, always, never, and other absolutist notions) are typically irrational because, by definition, virtually nothing in life conforms to such commands.*

*Some other versions of irrational thoughts consist of the variety: I can't stand something; it would be horrible if something occurred; I am totally worthless because I have not done something perfectly. While these thoughts do not contain the words "must" or "should" they are irrational because they are absolutist and untrue. Judging oneself on the basis of a success or failure is irrational—we are not reducible to our performance in tomorrow's show. To think in such absolute terms takes an incorrect view of who we are and places an exaggerated and, therefore, untrue importance on a single event.*

*It is crucial to understand the negative role that irrational thoughts play in our lives: Irrational thoughts create emotional distress—disturbed emotions that are disproportionate to the things or events about which we are concerned. The goal of REBT is not to eradicate emotions, but rather to alter debilitating and unproductive levels of emotion. The goal of REBT is to replace irrational thoughts with rational ones, which will better serve our emotional health as well as assist us in attaining our goals.*

**CHAPTER 6**

# RATIONAL vs IRRATIONAL THINKING

*I think facing reality [is important], when people are pressing themselves, and it's not working. I think they have to sit down and really take a deep look at the situation, at how things really are. You know you can think one thing, but it could be going another way."*

~ Rodney Jenkins

In order to determine whether a risk is right for you, you need to develop a clear understanding of yourself. Unfortunately, many of us have unrealistic views of ourselves, which inhibit our ability to attain our goals.

In this chapter, we will show you how to look at yourself realistically so that you can find your true abilities and begin using them to your best advantage.

### BREAKING THE CYCLE

People gain a sense of who they are and what capabilities they possess by learning. People learn through several means:

- By their own experiences.
- By examining the experiences of others.
- By encouragement or discouragement from others.

• By interpreting how their body feels (nerves) in any given situation.

All our learning experiences are sifted or screened by our own idiosyncratic "glasses," which constitute our very own way of seeing the world. Our so-called glasses influence how we learn and lead us to form habits about how we think of ourselves.

These learned habits of thinking influence what challenges we pursue and what ones we avoid. They also influence how much effort we will expend toward attaining a goal and how long we will persist in search of it. In other words, one person may be willing to continue despite a lengthy struggle, while another might be more prone to quitting when success does not come quickly.

Over time, we learn and develop these habits of thinking through our experiences. The more experiences we have, the more information we have to base our thinking on. Although learning is an ongoing process, we often become caught in one particular habit or way of thinking that greatly influences not only our confidence, but also the degree of fear we feel whenever we face new challenges.

We need to learn how to break this cycle of negative thinking in order to intelligently and clearly assess our abilities so that

*A model of the learning and interpretive process that develops and influences the way people act:*

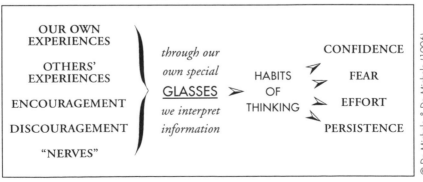

we may achieve our goals.

Although the guiding theory of this book, Rational Emotive Behavior Therapy (REBT) sounds complex, it has a simple message. It proposes that people are motivated by a basic desire to stay alive and to be happy. Sometimes, however, people get in their own way of trying to achieve those goals by assigning blame, either to themselves or to others, instead of seeking the truth when things do not meet their own unrealistic standards.

Most people don't realize that they have a choice of which glasses to wear as learning filters. Most do not realize that they are the ones who ultimately decide whether to believe those things about themselves that are simply untrue (*irrational thoughts*), or base their beliefs on reality (*rational thoughts*). Wearing distorted glasses can curtail a person's pursuit of happiness because it leads them to perceive inaccurate information. It blinds them to the real challenges and leads them to ignore their own real abilities.

On the other hand, looking at life through clear and undistorted lenses can help people to pursue their own personal happiness because it allows them to see things as they really are. This is known as rational thinking, and those who employ it will have a better chance at success because they will have accurate information to prepare, to set goals, and to decide strategies.

## IRRATIONAL THINKING

Most of us do think irrationally from time to time. It is a part of human nature. But chronic, irrational thinking can produce disastrous results. Irrational thinking usually manifests itself as some absolutist belief like, "If I don't win today, I am terrible." This type of thinking often causes us to misinterpret challenges and experiences not only in the present, but in the future. For example, if you didn't win last Tuesday's jumping event, irrational thinking may encourage you to become even more fearful about future competitions. Such negative thinking can actually hinder your future performance.

It is a paradox of human nature that people seek pleasure by attaining goals, yet they often sabotage those very same goals by their irrational thinking. Dwelling on self-blame will not help you solve problems nor will it help achieve your goals. If you convince yourself that you are a terrible rider simply because you don't always win; or that if you get injured, you will surely die, you will simply increase the tension you feel and often, escalate the amount of fear you experience. Time is better spent solving the problem. When people are thinking irrationally they beat themselves up for poor performances and nag themselves for little mistakes. They look for the failures within themselves and use those as examples of why they are no good at what they want to do. When they fall, or nearly fall, or see others fall, they catastrophize what they see and think of imminent death or disability. When people are thinking irrationally, they are in effect, carrying on a negative mental conversation with themselves. This internal dialogue reinforces feelings of failure by constantly practicing harmful thoughts. Like exercising a muscle, repetition builds fitness, and people get quite fit at beating themselves up. The whole process becomes a highly skilled, well-learned bad habit of self-abasement—one that is founded on false information gleaned through those distorted glasses they have learned to wear.

## SELF TALK

People who think irrationally engage in a harmful internal dialogue with themselves called self-talk. In this negative self-talk they tell themselves that they *must* meet certain criteria (imposed by themselves or others) to be worthwhile. They threaten themselves by believing that failure in any small part to achieve that image of perfection constitutes total failure.

As you can see, thinking negative thoughts is not the way to get past your fears, nor is it the way to go after what you want in riding. Irrational thoughts will only serve to ruin your enjoyment of the sport and your performance.

*Irrational thoughts are part of a vicious four-step cycle:*

Chronic nagging and self-abusive self-talk lead to a pressure to win every time or to meet one's own perfectionistic standards. In turn, these pressures and fears result in poor performances caused by self-induced emotional distress. Likewise, poor performances lead to further feelings of failure and even worse self-abusive inner dialogues. Clearly, it is a destructive cycle.

Irrational thoughts cloud the real issues, making it difficult to find the next logical step to take toward improving your ability, minimizing the risk, and closing in on personal goals.

## HOW TO THINK RATIONALLY

In contrast, a rationally thinking rider knows what she wants out of the sport (victory, camaraderie, etc.) and what she doesn't want (injury, poor performances, etc.). She learns that she can strive for the things she wants with a sense of *hopeful realism* about meeting her goals.

Hopeful realism is the non-demanding expectation that one has some, but not total, control over the outcome of an event. It is the mature understanding that there are some things one can change, such as your thoughts and your actions, and some things one cannot control, such as outcomes and many aspects of the external world.

When a rationally thinking rider loses a competition, she can walk away from the experience and analyze it logically. She can pick out the best parts of the performance and feel good, and she can pick out the worst parts and try to figure out how to fix them next time. Most importantly, she can critique the performance without catastrophizing that she is all bad, or that the performance was all bad.

*A rationally thinking rider can critique herself without self-abusive criticism.* She can pick out the good and the bad without feeling that she should have done better and that she is terrible and a complete failure. The rationally thinking rider does not entertain such irrational thoughts.

*Rational thoughts are a part of a positive cycle that can lead to success:*

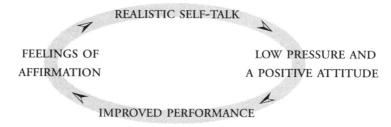

REALISTIC SELF-TALK

FEELINGS OF
AFFIRMATION

LOW PRESSURE AND
A POSITIVE ATTITUDE

IMPROVED PERFORMANCE

Engaging in realistic self-talk leads to decreased pressure and a positive attitude toward your goals. Effort and concentration can increase, leading to improved performances, which further affirm the realistic self-talk based on positive experiences.

**GET REAL**

If you choose to wear distorted glasses, you are choosing to put yourself down and make yourself miserable by demanding the impossible. You cannot be perfect. Nobody can. But a hopefully realistic person can work toward increasing their chances of success by setting certain realistic goals and then pursuing them.

One common irrational myth is that some people "have it," and some people, "just don't." People who think irrationally often lump themselves into the "just don't" category. This sort of thinking serves as a devious excuse not to try anything and stems from an irrational belief that life should be easy. It isn't. In a rational view, discomfort is seen as a part of being alive.

## THE CHALLENGE

| RATIONAL | IRRATIONAL |
|---|---|
| Focuses on what's important and ways around the situation | Focuses on the unfairness of the situation |
| Examines what things can be controlled (in the situation and in attitude toward the situation) | Gets lost in things that can't be controlled |
| Ranks the things that can be controlled, and attacks the ones that will make the biggest difference | Fails to identify the internal (mental) and external (situational) elements that can solve problem |
| Thinks about using the situation to its best advantage— to get as close to the goal as possible | Stays stuck in what was wanted and misses ways to make the best of the current situation . . . Mourns the loss of perfection |
| Thinks how successes and failures can be used to improve | Seeks success but has trouble attaining it because of fear of failure and feelings of no control and worthlessness or shame |

## THE RESULTS

| CONFIDENCE | FEAR |
|---|---|
| Takes on healthy challenges | Avoids healthy challenges |
| Works hard to improve and find solutions | Goes "through motions" feeling failure is imminent |
| Continues when the going gets tough because he/she "knows there *will* be a way" | Quits when things gets tough because he/she "knows there *isn't* any way" |
| Enjoys riding, with maximized potential and attainment of goals | Feels bitter, leading to reduced potential and avoidance of goals |

Ironically, those who are willing to face the discomforts that stand in their way, will go the farthest, and be the most comfortable with their achievements.

If you want to succeed, you need to look rationally at what is needed in order to overcome your fears and meet challenges along the way. No doubt, you will see that hard work is the most important ingredient for success in horseback riding and talent the least important. Many people have good genes, but not everyone can do the work. Great riders are incredible people precisely because they are ordinary people. They love what they are doing so much that they are willing to devote enormous mental and physical effort to pursue their goals and dreams. The hard work they do to stay on top of their game is a lesson that debunks the irrational thought that pursuing the things you want in life must be easy. If you can be honest with yourself and your surroundings, then you too will be able to progress steadily toward your goals for you will be fighting the real battles instead of fighting with yourself.

In dealing with reality you should be very objective about:
- Your abilities.
- The abilities of your horse(s).
- The rigors of the challenges you face.

The top riders we interviewed all were quick to point out that the way to pursue their dreams and minimize the risk involved was to deal with the real facts. They all had goals that they pursued with a firm sense of reality. They were all very successful, and very rational.

Bruce Davidson has enjoyed his sport and attained a great success in it through a tremendous amount of hard work. He exemplifies the kind of life philosophy this book is all about. Davidson, a five-time Olympian, was also named United States Combined Training Associations Rider of the Year 14 times. Below he explains his attitude toward work.

"I picked a job I liked. I knew that I would work all my

*Five-time Olympian Bruce Davidson says that hard work is the key to success.*

life. Everybody needs a job. When I was a young boy my father told me that if you want to be happy you must pick a job and work at it. If you like it or not you still have to work. If you want to be the best doctor, lawyer, painter, musician, or anything, you have got to do it eight days a week 25 hours a day. And it takes that much. And it takes that same kind of dedication if you want to be the greatest farmer. You have to work at it."

~ Bruce Davidson

The riders interviewed in this book, these ordinary folks from different backgrounds and disciplines, all became great through hard work, diligence, and tenacity. Their habits can be yours too if you are willing to read how these great people think, find where you want to go, and are diligent in listening to yourself and debating with yourself on the accuracy of what your brain is telling you. You will be amazed at the difference when you stop nagging yourself and just get real!

## MENTAL SKILLS FOR THRILLS AND SPILLS

If you know where you want to go, and you are motivated to get there, but are still experiencing disturbing fear or concern, a few mental exercises may help you. Before we proceed, it is important to understand two things. First, that the mind and body are hard-wired together. What goes on in one affects the other. It is a myth that the two are separate. Second, that nothing succeeds like success. In this section, we will help you practice defeating challenges, both mentally and physically, in order to build your confidence.

As Greg Ryan says about this process, it can be very liberating and exciting. "You overcame your fear. Now that's a high! You challenged it and you overcame it. You feel good, and that's a wonderful thing."

## CHAPTER 7

# DEFEATING

# IRRATIONAL THINKING

## A PRACTICAL GUIDE

*I've learned through trial and error to transform negative energy into positive excitement. . . . For example, begin to look forward to the "up" feeling before a performance, label the "butterflies" as excitement rather than fear, look forward to the chance to rise to another level.*

~ Greg Best

Everyone has irrational thoughts that get in the way of their goals. Irrational thoughts are often streams of mental garbage that interfere with how you feel about yourself and the things that you want to try.

By carefully listening to your own head, you will see that perhaps you've had negative conversations with yourself, and that many of these conversations are filled with self-nagging, self-doubting, and self-downing thoughts.

The way to turn yourself off of these self-defeating thoughts is to:

- Listen to yourself and debate yourself all the time.

- Be your own lawyer and expose the weakness of your own mind's case.

The biggest case against irrational thoughts is that they are absolutist. They demand that you must, should, or have to do or be something, or else you are an absolute failure. When you start hearing those demands in your head, you know you have a war to wage with your mind!

As a human being in this world, it is likely that you have recognized that things don't always go the way you want them to go. Rodney Jenkins and Valerie Kanavy both admit that sometimes, "It just isn't your day." As a matter of fact, it is practically a law of nature that some days will be better than others.

Everyone has good and bad days. Olympians fall off. Inexperienced riders from out of nowhere win top competitions. There is no such thing as a sure thing, an absolute. Knowing that, it is irrational to hold yourself to such a standard.

## ABSOLUTE STANDARDS

The best riders know that there are no absolute standards of how things should be. Absolute standards are the core beliefs that can make you miserable if you allow yourself to subscribe to them. They consist of irrational absolute "musts" and "shoulds" as standards of self-judgment. Below are several ways to help you attack this type of thinking.

- When you say, "I must be a perfect rider," you are setting yourself up for misery. Perfect riders don't exist." Let's say you're waiting your turn to enter the show ring. You say to yourself, "I'll look like a fool if I ride before all those people." Attack it by saying "STOP. Every top rider has made mistakes and looked stupid. Everybody has seriously messed up at one time or another, and that must make my thought an absolutist belief too."

- Another way to attack these negative thoughts is to pretend that your best friend is listening to you beat yourself up with all this irrational, illogical thinking. Likely, your best friend would be horrified. He or she would not be able to stand by and listen to you abuse yourself with the unrealistic, absolutist demands you're putting on yourself. The friend would surely debate your flawed logic and point out all the good things you have done as examples of why you are not so terrible. Therefore, try to act as if you were your own best friend. Try to give yourself that kind of rational support.

• Talk to people who are good at what they do, and ask them about mistakes they made in the past. Everybody makes them—not just beginners. By talking to these veterans you can see that they make as many, and sometimes more mistakes than other people—but they also understand that it is a part of the game. They don't let it get them down. They learn and they move on. The ones who learn and get past their mistakes the fastest are the ones who see the world realistically . . . and get right back on track and think rationally.

Leslie Webb is a great dressage rider, but she relates some great mess up stories that illustrate this point quite well.

"I've had so many . . . so many completely embarrassing moments, that I wanted to crawl into the nearest hole and never come out. I mean, I can tell you once that I had someone reading to me [the dressage test] and I couldn't hear him, and I went off course five times. I mean that was embarrassing.

"I've told them [students] that I was so young and naive I didn't know really what to do. Rather than just turning to the judge and stopping and saying, 'excuse me,' and then turning to the reader and saying, 'I can't hear you!' Judges are human beings too. Or, [once I had] a reader read for me who got so in-tuned to what

I was doing and then forgot to read. That was embarrassing as well.

"I was a little bit more mature at that point and I stopped and looked at the judge, and said, 'excuse me but I don't know where I'm going so . . . ,' and I was looking right at my reader [when I said that]. I do remember going off course too, like memorizing the wrong test. It's so embarrassing. But it humbles you and it makes you work harder. When I make a mistake like that, I go home and work harder at home, and do more homework and really memorize my test. And that's what I try to tell them [the students]."

~ Leslie Webb

People are fallible. They make mistakes, even the best do. But when you practice dwelling on evidence that is self-damaging, you are helping yourself fail. As we've already stated, your mind and body are wired together, and if you convince yourself you can't do something, then you probably won't be able to. On the other hand, if you are logical about your thoughts, you will see that everyone makes mistakes, everyone falls, and everyone messes up. Life does not conform to our demands, and by making demands of it, you are setting yourself up for disappointment, fear of failure, and injury. It is all right to want something badly and to be a hopeful realist, but there is a difference between preference and demand. Demands are absolute, preferences are realistic.

As long as you remain an absolutist, an unrealistic judge of yourself, you will never feel free to go out and make the mistakes you need to make in order to learn and improve. You will always stand before your own self-created judge, head hung low, because you cannot meet your own unattainable standards of absolute perfection. You will never see failures as the little victories they really are. All the best riders fail, and all the best riders go on to ride the next day just a little bit wiser for the process.

In order to defend against irrational thoughts, you need to:

• Develop strong, sensible thinking. By examining the simple question, "How is this negative thought helping me do what I want?" you will begin to spot the flaws in your thoughts. Say to yourself, "There are no guarantees. Some days I may not be great and I may look foolish, but the only standard I need to meet is my own. I *prefer* to do well, and I would *prefer* that my practice shows up as a good performance, but I do not *demand* any of those things because demands require perfection, and that is impossible."

• Avoid the illogical expansion of one bad day (which everyone has) to you as a rider in general, or you as a person. Again, that is not logical, nor is it based on reality, and it most certainly won't help you attain success.

• Expose your own negative thoughts and beliefs by blowing them up to their huge and ridiculous extreme. Say, "You know, I'm absolutely right. I shouldn't have lost that stirrup. I'm so lousy that people should study me to learn how not to ride. I am the worst rider on the whole planet because of that one stirrup problem. In fact, I simply cannot go on because, who knows, some day I might lose another stirrup and who knows what would happen then . . . the world might stop spinning." You will quickly realize how ridiculous and irrational you are being.

It is clear that such demands don't work. Irrational thoughts and the negative self-talk that comes from being unrealistic and irrational about yourself will only damage your performance and prevent you from attaining your goals.

But by understanding and controlling these thoughts, you can influence the way you think, feel, and perform. You do not need to ride the wave of life passively. There are waves, but you can go under them, through them, or surf on top of them.

## MENTAL IMAGERY: THE MIND AND BODY

We showed you how to listen to your thoughts closely to find self-defeating comments you might be giving yourself, and how to debate and minimize them. Now we will take you on a mental exercise that will prepare you for using mental imagery.

Mental imagery is a powerful tool that not only activates the mind, but all your senses. By concentrating and literally practicing certain skills and strategies in your mind, your body learns how to perform those very skills. Imagery is not as good as actually practicing, but it works, and it can be used along with the other techniques we have discussed.

For instance, if you are waiting your turn to compete, you might use it to imagine how you will ride in that competition. This will not only help you to practice the test and memorize the course, it will also help you become confident and thus reduce your fear. Leslie Webb uses this technique prior to dressage competitions and suggests it for her students too.

> "I started doing a lot of focusing mentally on my performance . . . days before . . . and mentally really running through all of the tests. I think the most important time for me is . . . when I arrive at the showgrounds. I sit in front of the arena that I am competing in and literally run through my test and think about when I am extending my trot across the diagonal, what am I looking at. That's what I do, so that if I happen to get a little bit lost and I look up, that kind of helps me.

> "In my mind I'm on the horse doing it and I'm visually looking in the direction that . . . I would be [ during the test]. When I'm standing there in front of that arena, I make sure that when I run through it mentally, I never break my train of thought. If I break my train of thought once, then my homework is not being done, so I start over. If I can run through it mentally without breaking my train of thought, it must last as long as the test.

"What a lot of people say is to find the quietest place you can find and go over your test. I have told my students to go and find the busiest place and go do your test, because the dressage ring is never quiet. There is commotion everywhere, and that's helped with a couple of my students. That's a challenge, and if they can get through it without breaking their train of thought . . . then they're going to be ready for the dressage arena."

~ Leslie Webb

Mental imagery can also be used to help you handle unexpected problems. For example, you might try imagining strategies that will help you successfully deal with losing a stirrup or with a horse that misbehaves. Just imagine the situation and think about a successful response. By repeating this exercise over and over, you will become more confident, and your body and mind will become better prepared to handle any eventuality.

To a small degree, mental imagery actually activates your nerves and your muscles. It literally gives you a practice. Make no mistake, this is not simply daydreaming. It is purposeful, mental practice where the object is to mentally envision scenarios as vividly as possible (using all the senses). It entails going through a practice session, practicing your skills, and solving problems along the way. To illustrate the power of imagery, we will take you on a little mental trip designed to use all the senses. We recommend that you have someone read the following section to you, or that you read it into a tape recorder so that you may listen to it with your eyes closed while concentrating.

## USING ALL THE SENSES

Imagine that you see a large green ball. It is smooth and shiny. As you look at the ball it changes colors to red and then starts to bounce on the floor. It is now a red playground ball, and it is bouncing inside a log cabin. You are in the cabin alone on a hot day. The windows are all open and there is this red ball bouncing. It is making no noise at all, but you can feel the sweltering breeze through the open windows on this sunny day. The ball continues to bounce, and now you can hear it bouncing. It sounds like a basketball, and the sound becomes annoyingly loud. You look at the red bouncing ball and approach it. It is bouncing in front of you only a foot away, and you grab it and feel its rubbery red surface. You are holding the rubbery red ball on this hot, breezy, sunny day in a log cabin with open windows —when suddenly, you smell syrup and pancakes.

The smell comes from the right, so you turn to your right and see a hallway that has a single window at the end. You walk along the creaky floor toward the window and tuck the red ball under your left arm. The window at the end of the hall is open and you can see flags ruffling on long, silver poles outside. As you approach the window, you see to your left a door that is partly open, which leads to the warm breezy outside. Near the door is a table with pancakes and syrup. There is no chair so you stand near the table, put down the ball, which rolls out the door, and take the knife and the fork. You cut a small piece of the pancakes, which are stacked three high, and swish them in the syrup that has been poured all over them. You can smell the sweetness, and feel the steam of the pancakes on your face as you lean over and put a sweet fork full of syrupy pancakes in your mouth and eat it.

You hear a loudspeaker in the distance, so you put down the knife and fork and walk out the door in front of you. You see the ball right outside the door to your left, and you also see that, outside, the grass is a brilliant green and there are shady trees all around the small cabin. It is a very peaceful place, full of smells of flowers and cut grass and the warm lilting breezes from this sunny day. You feel amazingly calm and sleepy and sit down on the lush grass and take off your shoes. You can feel the grass tickle your toes as you lean back and close your eyes under a large shady tree. You are relaxed and happy about this quiet spot you have found. It feels safe and it is filled with happy noises of birds and the occasional bumblebee in the distance.

The loudspeaker in the distance sounds again, and you hear your name. The announcer is saying that this is your last call and that you have two minutes to get into the ring. You leap to your feet and look around, your heart is beating faster and faster, as you begin to sweat. The trees and the house disappear and you are standing, heart pounding, facing an enormous ring. You are standing before a stadium at the in-gate. You can smell the sand in the ring and hear your heart beating and feel the sweat trickle. It is hot, and you can smell the sand, and see a monstrous crowd waving banners and screaming. You are wearing your riding outfit, and your horse is beside you.

You hear the announcer call your name for the last call, and you are terrified. What is going on? Your heart is in your mouth and you can feel your legs turn rubbery. Your face is white as a sheet and your hands are cold and clammy. Your coach comes forward to give you a leg up, and says, "You look really pumped up . . . I can tell you're ready. This is for all the marbles!"

Suddenly you are on your horse entering the ring and the crowd starts shouting. You can feel the horse under you shake at the sight of the shouting, screaming spectators. You remember what your coach said, and you realize that this is the way great riders feel when they are ready. You smile and wave at the crowd, and they shout your name and stamp their feet in unison. The whole place is beating in rhythm and you feel the adrenaline pound in your brain and through your arms and legs. You feel the tingles and your heart beating faster, and you smile because you know you are ready. You feel great. You are at the Olympics . . . and the world is watching you . . . and you are ready. You feel like a live wire of excitement and strength and agility and power. The crowd is going wild, and you feel great.

The crowd quiets and gradually goes completely silent. Your coach walks into the ring and says, "That was excellent . . . you see nerves are good for you if you trust them . . . now go back to the cabin and relax."

You are standing by the pancakes again, right near the door. But they are cold, and all the adrenaline, even if it did feel good for a while, made you feel too sick to eat anyhow. So you go out under the tree again. There you spot a book and pick it up, and find yourself reading where we are right now.

## USING IMAGERY TO SOLVE PROBLEMS

By creating scenarios for yourself, you can become accustomed to the feeling of adrenaline as depicted in the example above. You can play with the way you interpret the nervous energy you feel through the type of imagery we used. We made it seem bad at first, and then altered the interpretation so it felt good at the end.

You can use mental imagery to practice skills and to help you become accustomed to those things you fear. Imagery can also help you by either gradually exposing you to larger and larger doses of the thing you fear, or by dumping the thing you fear on you in its entirety . . . like we did above. It is up to you to decide how to use mental imagery to your advantage. Imagery is a useful, safe learning tool.

Because the mind and the body are connected, irrational thoughts, images and fears can be defeated in either the mind or in the body. One will convince the other. If you have irrational fears of failure or injury, then the more you face either one, either by doing the thing you fear or by vividly imagining doing it, then the more that fear will dissipate. Every time you win a battle, you become stronger. In contrast, every time you run from an irrational fear, the fear becomes stronger.

Two ways of facing fears that often make use of imagery are *flooding* and *systematic desensitization*. Flooding entails going after the entire fearful situation and facing it (mentally and/or physically), all at once, like Greg Ryan did when he rode so soon after his injury. This may be a good method if you already have the physical skills and feel ready to confront your fears.

Systematic desensitization, on the other hand, entails a gradual confrontation of the thing you fear. By using relaxation techniques to keep you calm, you face a little more each day. Many of the great riders and coaches we have interviewed employ this method of gradual teaching as a part of their lessons.

The key component in both methods is to confront the fearful thing, either in large or in small parts. If an irrational fear stands in your way, you need to practice defeating it mentally and/or physically. The more times you succeed, the more the bad habit of fear will dissipate and the more the good habit of confidence will develop.

You will notice that we said that systematic desensitization encourages the use of using relaxation techniques in order to reduce nervous energy, while attacking the fearful activity. The argument for this method is that by being relaxed and facing the fear at the same time, the mind and body will learn a new habit. The feared task becomes associated with relaxation and, therefore, extinguishes the old habit and the nervous energy associated with the task.

Research has not been clear enough to demonstrate that relaxation is the key to success in defeating fears. As we presented earlier, it is our argument, supported by both a growing body of research and interviews with many successful riders, that nervous energy gets a bad reputation because people interpret it irrationally and decide that it is a negative thing. Greg Best says,

> "I've learned through trial and error to transform negative energy into positive excitement. The cognitive strategies [I use] are a kind of "relabeling" which means, in my terms, to try to find a positive aspect in a negative emotion. For example, begin to look forward to the "up" feeling before a performance, label the "butterflies" as excitement rather than fear, look forward to the chance to rise to another level...it is virtually impossible to tell yourself not to be nervous, or to end the anxiety through sheer will."
>
> ~ Greg Best

As numerous riders can attest, the nervous energy and the feeling of the unknown can be the most exciting parts of competing.

We encourage you to feel as nervous as you want. Feel it, accept it, flood yourself with it if necessary until you are sick of being afraid, and understand that you need it to help you beat the challenges you face. If you find that you are still too nervous to perform at your optimal level, go back to REBT and find those hidden irrational thoughts that are *maintaining* your fear.

## CHANGING NEEDS

As we have discussed, getting to know yourself is a big part of success in riding. This means many things, including getting to know what level of relaxation or excitement helps you perform best and helps you enjoy performing.

As you work to overcome your fears of riding, to get them to a manageable level where the excitement helps instead of hurts your performance, be aware that what is helpful to you may change from week to week, from day to day, and even from moment to moment during a ride.

## CHAPTER 8

# MOTIVATION:

## RUNNING AWAY FROM FAILURE

### OR

## RUNNING TOWARD SUCCESS

*The desire to ride can fly in the face of very serious fears, motivating, and ultimately enabling, the individual to work . . .*

~ John Lyons

You have to be motivated, and motivated for the right reasons, in order to overcome your fears and meet new challenges in riding. The motivation in top riders is phenomenal. They do it for themselves and they do not compare themselves to what or who they wish they were. They are motivated by their own standards, not those of others. Most important, they are motivated by their own joy in learning.

### RIDING FOR THE RIGHT REASONS

Even if you don't aspire to be a top rider, if you know yourself well, are motivated by the joy of the sport, have a direction, and then pursue it piece by piece, you will learn more, have less fear, and enjoy your riding more.

Those who live for each day, who get up in the morning excited to do their sport, are the people who will learn more, and hurdle over more tough patches. They will see each day as a chance to improve, and they will appreciate and enjoy all the success they have experienced each step of the way.

In contrast, those who are chasing some false image of perfection, some model of the perfect ride or the ever-important award, will spend each day trying to push their imperfect selves a little closer toward their goal, chastising themselves all along the way. After just a short while, that can become demoralizing.

Great riders like Bruce Davidson know that winning is just one kind of proof of having done a good job in the training. He also knows that the training is where one's motivation should lie, not in the reward at the end. That is a difficult task in a culture obsessed with winning. If all you want is the victory, then training becomes a fearful thing. It is something you have to do in order to get what you want.

If you really crave victory more than anything, you will live in constant fear of defeat. If you crave victory more than the sport itself, you will be more willing to ride horses and courses for which you are not prepared. You will experience more fear of failure and more fear of getting hurt, because you will have had more actual failures and more actual injuries than you would have had you been more selective with the challenges you attempted. There will also be a motivational fight that goes on inside your mind. You will ask yourself, do I love winning enough to do these challenging things? Do I want to do this one more week, one more month, one more year, before I can't stand it anymore?

This brings us back to the idea of hopeful realism. When you are motivated to improve, not just win, it is easier to look at what you and your horse really have going for you. From that point, you can:

• Build a plan to get to where you want to go.

- Begin to take measures to push yourself (one realistically hopeful step at a time) into new territory.
- Physically and mentally challenge yourself.

When you love what you are doing and you know where you are going, fears become minor little setbacks, trying times that you turn into learning experiences.

Bruce Davidson is one of the best, most consistent performers ever to ride a horse. He believes that,

> "When people are doing what they really want to do . . . the fear goes away. It is the day-to-day process that is the reward. If all they want is the Olympics, then I pray they don't make it. They are making it just to make it. Always try to beat yourself, not others."
>
> ~ Bruce Davidson

Riding is a dangerous enough sport without making it worse by taking chances that are not useful to where you want to go. According to some statistics riding is the most dangerous sport in the world. The best riders in the world know this better than anyone. When a horse, a course, or a situation does not suit them, they will get off the horse, exit the competition, or leave the situation faster than any beginner, when faced with a realistically insurmountable challenge.

## MOTIVATED BY FEAR

Unfortunately, many riders willingly expose themselves to danger by striving to prove that they are not scared, when, in fact, they are. Any motivation, driven by fear of failure or letting those around you down, is not a strong enough motive to keep you in riding for the long haul. Motivation by fear can do a great job for a while, but it can wear you down and cause you to quit. A perfect example of the incredible power of motivation by fear can be found in the story below about the Civil War.

On July 16, 1861, Union troops set out from Washington, D.C., and made a two-day, 24-mile march to reach Manassas, Virginia. On the 21st, the Union and Confederate troops clashed. Confederate troops were victorious, and the Union, fleeing for their lives, retreated back to Washington, D.C., covering the same 24 miles in less than half a day.

Fear made these individuals perform far above their normal abilities. They had great motivation, instilled by fear, to accomplish a next-to-impossible feat. Had they been required to continue at that almost inhuman pace, their success would surely have been short-lived.

Motivation by fear is a limited thing. It might result in a freak episode of success, but guaranteed and consistent success can only be achieved by those who are genuinely motivated by the love of their sport, and who prove their motivation by preparation.

Many times fear comes head-to-head with the desire to appear good, which can also lead to accidents. Experienced coaches, friends and trainers are crucial resources for beginners who are just figuring out their abilities.

Below, Carol Lavell describes a typical conversation that she has had time and time again while working with riders.

> ". . . she [a student] says, 'I'm afraid he [the horse] is going to do that to me again.' And I say 'I'm afraid he's going to do that again and we need to find someone to straighten your horse out so that he doesn't hurt you . . . And, if the horse starts it again then we have another option, and it's called sell the horse.'"
>
> ~ Carol Lavell

You should realize that getting hurt only slows your progress, no matter wherever it is you are trying to get (unless your goal is to get hurt or to look tough). If you are on a horse who is a winner for someone else, but is proving too much for you to handle at this stage in your training, get another mount.

If you are in a situation you feel is over your head, stop and get help from someone more experienced.

Often people become fixated on comparing themselves to others, or comparing themselves to where they think they ought to be. They scare themselves with self-threats about milestones they must reach and awards they must accomplish to be good riders. These people shine the spotlight of their focus on the wrong targets.

## MOTIVATED TO LEARN

The motivation to learn and be their best has led some riders like Bruce Davidson, Rodney Jenkins, and others to recognize the necessity of the far more involved and challenging process that goes beyond simply taking lessons. They, and others like them, have recognized that to be really great at what they want to do involves the horse as a part of the whole leaning process. They and other successful riders, not only train themselves as riders, but they also train their horses as well.

The training makes them better riders, and it makes their horses trained specifically for them. It is a win-win situation that takes time, and no person who is in it for just a medal would ever pursue training their own horses. It would be too much work and take too much time. Their motivation would die when it was overcome by waves of fear of failure or injury, and would finally result in burnout.

Successful riders are motivated people who have gone farther in their sport than most ever have or ever will. That is because they know what it takes to be great. Being great is all about being motivated to get up in the morning and do the thing you love, meeting whatever challenges the day poses with the patience and courage of a person who knows that this is what he or she really wants to be doing.

Our experts like Jenkins and Davidson have figured this out. They enjoy their sport and are not fixated on winning. Remember, these are the same experts who win the most.

## CHAPTER 9

# FINDING YOUR PATH

*If you don't know where you are going, then how are you going to get there?"*

Leslie Webb

Dreams are what govern the overall direction that successful people take in life. Dreams are the incredible thoughts people have of themselves doing exactly what they've always wanted to do. Those who chase their dreams and set goals to get there are among the happiest people in the world. Chasing a dream is an exciting and frightening thing: exciting because pursuing it gives life direction and meaning; frightening because there is no guarantee of success. Dreams require motivation, determination, and focus in a highly personal direction that others may not understand.

### HAVING A DREAM

Dreams are the compass by which people set their goals. Unfortunately, they often get pushed aside for other things that are more important to the moment, or that are more important to other people. Picking a direction is one of the first steps to figuring out what risks in riding you should and should not take. Having a direction gives reason to every challenge you take as you move toward your destination.

Dreams answer the big question, Why am I doing any of

this? The answer to a question like that is easy when you are fervently pursuing your dreams—because you love what you are doing.

When tough times arrive, as they surely will, riders who love what they are doing always have the upper hand. They will have more motivation to keep going. Western horseman, author and trainer John Lyons is renowned for his ability in training difficult horses and for helping riders prevent and overcome their fears. As he puts it, "At times it seems a paradox. . . . Why do what you fear? And then you remember the answer . . . Because you love it."

## THE IMPORTANCE OF GOALS

Great riders make plans and pick goals for themselves that will give them a chance at their dreams. They've learned that competitions are won with skills, and that skills are won with practice, and for them, that practice is a labor of love. In fact, it is precisely this striving that gives life meaning. The greatest thing in the world is not necessarily getting what you want, but knowing what you want, and then working to get it.

Rodney Jenkins, in his 35 years in show jumping, has won more Grand Prix (78) than anybody else in the United States. Given such success, one could assume he has achieved all his goals.

If that were true, he might have quit the horse world already, but he hasn't. In order to continue enjoying the horses and the business, he has picked new goals and redefined his dreams.

Today, as a steeplechase trainer, he is, as he puts it, "a little fish in a big pond." He has picked goals that are both challenging and attainable, the mark of a true hopeful realist. He has picked a new sport (steeplechasing), in which he had always had an interest, and decided to try and master it. Jenkins knew that he needed to set new goals in order to grow and succeed and to stay happy.

"I'm as happy now as I've ever been in my whole life.
Now I can go to the races and do a stable of race horses
and I like it. I'm not as good at it [as with the show
jumpers], but I still like it. It is like a whole new career.
I've got something. I'm a little fish in a big pond now,
like I was when I started showing. It really gave me a
whole new life."

~ Rodney Jenkins

Being successful was great and, he says, "Now that I've had
a career that I did well in, I don't have to look back and say, 'I
could have been.' " He had already gotten where he wanted to
go, so he picked out something new. "When you're starting a
new venture, it really makes you get up and hustle." Getting
there is tremendous fun . . . as long as you like where you are
going.

## SETTING YOUR SIGHTS TOWARD YOUR DREAMS

Those riders who pick their own dreams and goals and choose
their own route to obtain them can count on two things. First,
they will learn more and take healthier risks because they will be
doing what they want to do. And second, they can count on
some people giving them a hard time and telling them that they
are wrong for what they are doing. As Rodney Jenkins puts it,

"Don't you think you've got to do what suits you? And
you know what? If you're a winner nobody is going to
bother you."

~ Rodney Jenkins

Dreams are highly personal. Knowing your dream helps you
set personal goals. Making each step on your own road to success
can be tough, especially when others complain they don't understand your particular style or approach. Remember that life is
your own personal experiment and that part of the fun of living
it is trying things out and chasing the things you love. Rigid

rules that dictate what to do and how to do it are for people who need more guidance, not for those who know where they are going. Those who know where they are going are flexible. They experiment to find out what works best for them.

Jenkins is an example of someone who always knew where he wanted to go. Ever willing to experiment, he refused to succumb to rigid rules about riding. He succeeded while using an unusual jumping style that openly confronted the norm of a sport that sells perfect form as the goal for all riders. Jenkins's comments about his style and the freedom he had to pursue his own training are powerful words which support the idea that there is no one way to get where you want to go. There are as many ways as there are people. But remember that your way is the best way for you. Be an active experimenter in your training.

> "Look at me [Jenkins says, pointing to a competition picture]. I'm off to the side. I'm back with my legs. But you know what? It was always the way I could balance the horse. It was how he left the ground . . . and I made sure I never interfered. That's what it is all about. It was no beauty contest. It is how you find a way to do what suits you best. The fear of what they think you look like doesn't matter because you are going to make them like the way you ride if you win enough. Nobody is turning kids loose and letting them learn to ride. To me, all the riders that have come up when I was showing didn't really have trainers. They were turned loose to school and ride themselves. Sure we all had help. But you learned to ride from practice. I had a field hunter and I had these bushes in the field. I'd go out every day after school and jump those bushes 5,000 times. I practiced timing."
>
> ~ Rodney Jenkins

Jenkins was turned loose to ride and to pursue his dreams. It can be difficult to have that freedom. Learn to be honest with yourself about what you want in life. Then convince yourself to overcome the risk of failing in order to get what you want.

Learn how to become a hopeful realist and see how someone like yourself can get from here to there by battling obstacles that get in the way such as other peoples' opinions and interferences and your own irrational thoughts. This can prove to be difficult as people will often try to convince you that your dreams are getting in the way of what they want you to do.

Being brave enough to go after what you want in riding may be hard. Most people are used to having others tell them what goals to pursue and what dreams they should chase. It is difficult to strike out in your own direction and do your own thing precisely because it may differ from what people around you want you to love.

There are pressures to win, or at least act like you want to win, and pressures to please other people and follow their advice. Often, this desire to please others is so strong that when someone speaks up on their own behalf to support their own direction in life, it can create confusion or friction with coaches, trainers, and others.

Below, well-known horse trainer and popular clinician John Lyons relates a story that captures this point quite well. It is an anecdote about a woman who had different goals than most in the sport. The woman left Lyons stumped at first.

> "During one of my clinics, I was approached by a woman in her thirties who had not had much experience with horses and had purchased a horse as a completely green yearling. Her interactions with the yearling had resulted in numerous crashes and minor accidents. When I began working with the owner, I asked if the horse had been halter broken. She began to demonstrate her successful halter "training" technique which consisted of dropping the halter into the feed bucket and attempting quickly to fasten the thing on

the horse's head when he dipped down to investigate the possibility of feed. The horse was much too fast for her. His assessment of, 'No feed,' was made before the halter was in place. He took off with her in tow, stepping on her slightly as he ran, and leaving her in tears on the ground.

"At first, I launched into a gentle lecture about haltering techniques, when the woman burst out with the question that was uppermost in her mind. "John, do I have to ride it?" Speechless, I listened as my client described her high stress job and the pleasure and release she experienced when she came to the barn to feed her horse. Her pleasure consisted of sitting on a milk stool to watch him enjoy his meal. Finally, I told her she was right—she didn't have to ride it. The horse fulfilled a particular need in the woman's life. As long as she felt no pressure to ride it, she enjoyed coming to the barn each day to feed and groom her horse, and to arrange for worming, shoeing, and vet care as necessary. The horse got great care as long as his owner felt no need to ride. If she felt pressure to ride that horse, she avoided the barn because being there made her feel guilty."

~ John Lyons

If you're shaking your head in disapproval at this gutsy woman's honesty with herself and her attainment of happiness, imagine how hard it will be to chase your own dreams, for you may face the same disapproval. Dreams and the goals you set are highly personal. No one will understand them as well as you.

But when you pursue your own personal goal regardless of its direction, some of the fears and pressures will begin to disappear, just like that woman's. As soon as she began doing what she wanted, which was enjoying her horse, the guilt and fear went away.

*Bruce Davidson, the only back-to-back world champion in eventing history, says that you need to love every day if you want to go far in any sport.*

## THE MEASURE OF SUCCESS

Bruce Davidson has no fear of failing in eventing because he loves it, and when you really love what you are doing, you can't wait for each new day. If you love your sport and the dream you are chasing, then success will come in two ways. It will come from doing what you love, and it will come from striving and achieving.

"My advice," says Davidson, "Is that if you are truly involved in the sport, then it is something that you will be taking part in for a lifetime . . . and if you are in it for a lifetime, then you will have success."

The end result, winning, qualifying, whatever, is clearly desirable, but it is not the sweetest part of success. That is reserved for the pleasure that comes from succeeding at each small goal along the way. And in so doing, becoming stronger and more confident in your chosen sport. If you are into riding for the long term, you will have the opportunity to experience a lifetime of enjoyable days, and know many successes.

## DEVELOP A PLAN

Take the time to examine what you really want from riding and develop a plan to achieve your goal. By having a destination in mind, and by planning how to get there, it will become clear to you that certain things (some of which are difficult and/or frightening) may need to be accomplished to get where you want to go. Many times an ingenious person can find a way to get to the destination, to reach the dream in a way that is different than the norm. Rodney Jenkins may not have been as good if he had been sold on the idea that form was the only way to succeed. When you know where you are going, you can experiment with different things that work best for you to get there.

Every successful rider has traveled a different path. They were all born with certain gifts and certain challenges. They learned different techniques and styles, but they all arrived at the same place. Watch, talk to, and seek out knowledgeable people who strike you as similar to yourself, in an effort to understand how to face challenges, overcome fears, and succeed.

The destination people choose has a strong influence on the challenges that need to be faced. Most people never pick where they are going, so they never know what they should be doing and what challenges they should or should not face. They simply ride around without a destination in mind.

Would you hop in a car and drive around aimlessly for years without a final destination in mind without so much as a map to get there? That is precisely what many people do in riding. They have not established a destination (dream) and have not established any goals (a roadmap). These same people then wonder why they are not succeeding nor being fulfilled by their riding.

People who don't know where they are going often have

questions about the risks they are taking, and rightly so. Some fear and pressure comes from pursuing goals which are not truly your own.

Take some time to examine what you truly want out of riding. Do not allow other people to dictate what direction you take and what your goals should be. Chart your own course. Then you will be able to answer the questions that arise along the way. You will always be able to say that the next challenge is logical because it is what you have to do to get what you want.

## BRAINSTORMING FOR SUCCESS

To find your destination, you should think about all the possible reasons you have for participating in riding. Write down what you like about the sport. Everyone likes to have fun, even top riders. So what makes you enjoy riding?

There are as many different reasons for riding as there are people. As we said before, everyone likes to win, but there are other things about riding that make people happy. Think carefully about all the many aspects of your sport: the way it makes you feel, the friends you meet, how fit you feel, the excitement, the achievement, and the competition. Write them all down on a list and rank everything in descending order beginning with what you like the most and continuing on with those things of lesser interest.

Now, make a list of all the things that bother you about riding. Write down the things you dislike because they are scary, or things that are just a pain, or that don't make any sense to you, or that really tick you off. Write down anything that bothers you about the sport. Then rank those in the same manner, from the worst to the least offensive.

With the two lists in hand, you now have a miniature summary of the pros and cons of your riding participation. Now, it is time to determine if they have any connections.

## WHAT I LIKE/DON'T LIKE ABOUT RIDING

PROS

CONS

*Examples*
Winning
Friendships
Competitions
Fitness
Mentally uplifting
Excitement
Achievement

*Examples*
Losing
Fear
Performance anxiety
I'm not fit enough
Mentally taxing
Butterflies
Fear of failure

_____          _____

_____          _____

_____          _____

_____          _____

_____          _____

_____          _____

_____          _____

_____          _____

_____          _____

_____          _____

_____          _____

_____          _____

_____          _____

_____          _____

_____          _____

_____          _____

## CONSTRUCTING GOALS

The brainstorming exercise gave you a glimpse into all the things you love and hate about riding. Now it is time to think carefully about where you want to go with riding in the long run. Ask yourself what kinds of things you like about riding? Can you think of any aspect of the sport that you could pursue to maximize these pleasurable experiences while minimizing your dislikes? Would the challenge of competition, the peace of trail rides, the camaraderie of team sports, or something you hadn't even thought of before satisfy those cravings?

Once you have sharpened your focus on where you want to go, nothing is insurmountable. It just takes a real love of where you are headed, a motivation to get there, and some planning for the steps that will lead you to your goal. Take some time, sit down, and find your direction.

Ask yourself, What do you really want out of riding? Are you looking to master your skills, to compete, or just for an enjoyable way to get some exercise? Where are you going? Once you begin to see a pattern in the things you love, you can set some goals to get there, and begin crossing off some things you hate. You will also start to see that some of the things you hate about riding may be things you might need to learn to work through or around, in order to achieve your goal.

Goals are the concrete steps you use to take on challenges, and they lead to lofty dreams. By setting goals, your fears and challenges can be broken down into small parts and conquered bit by bit. Riders often assume other people's goals (e.g., their coaches') as their own in an effort to accomplish difficult things. Sometimes these goals are mutual, and sometimes they are exclusively those of the coach. Even if a rider has no stake in a goal, she can still accomplish it because she has a plan.

If having goals and a direction in life (even if they are imposed by others) are both so powerful that they can lead to success at things you have no interest in, then imagine what will happen if you use them to pursue your dreams!

*Valerie Kanavy says that she might be a great endurance rider but that she is quick to get rid of bad horses. They are not an acceptable risk for where she wants to go in riding.*

## REACHING YOUR POTENTIAL

By now you have determined what you enjoy most about riding by identifying your own particular likes and dislikes, and have forced yourself to consider from that list where you can find your niche in the sport. Having picked your direction, now take some time to lay out your goals. This will give you an advantage over almost every other rider because:

- You will know why you are taking risks.
- You will have a map, made up of goals, to get you to your final destination, your dream.

While setting your goals, be a hopeful realist. *Hopeful* in that you are eagerly working toward the future by continually stretching your abilities and those of your horse and a realist in that you are looking squarely at *who* you are, *what* you want, and the way things *really* are.

Every small stretch you make entails an element of chance. There is the risk that you will not be realistic enough and will push too far, or not push far enough. There is the risk that you are not good enough, or that you will get hurt, or that others will see you fail.

But, when you make hopefully realistic goals, those risks become smaller and more sensible. They make sense on the road to your goals and dreams. Doing something you love will make you more tenacious in conquering each new goal along the way to your dream. You will put out more effort, take on tougher things, and persist longer in whatever you choose because you now have a stake in it. You've chosen the direction and you've set the goals. And, in the end, you will have enjoyed the fight, whether successful or not, because you will have tried your best in something you really love to do.

If you have done everything in your power and have not reached your dream, you can still sleep well at night knowing you have done something that almost no one ever does. You will have reached your potential. You truly are a success because you challenged yourself and took the chance.

## ONE STEP AT A TIME

Just as dreams have a better chance of coming true if good, logical, stepping-stone goals are constructed toward their attainment, so, too, do goals have a better chance of being attained if they not only consider the *product* (the end result, i.e., victory) you are seeking, but are constructed by building *process goals* (skills) within them.

Process goals are the little pieces that make up a successful goal performance. They are the skills you can measure. They mean having a more consistent crest-release in the hunters, they mean tighter turns and faster starts in barrel racing, they mean having a better ability to ride lines in cross-country. They mean rounder twenty-meter circles, and more contact in dressage. Process goals allow you to control the pieces and measure your success in controlling them fairly objectively. In contrast you cannot always control the product or measure how close you are to getting it.

As an example, let's say that your dream is to ride well in a Grand Prix dressage event and achieve a 60s score. Dressage competitions consist of a series of skills tests, each one progressively more difficult than the next. Scoring well on each successive test is very much like a series of process goals. Mastering each skill level will ultimately lead you to the highest level and your dream, a top-notch Grand Prix performance.

Those tests on the way to the top are not completely under our control because they rely on outcomes (the product) at each level to define success. To have the best control, and measure your progress the most accurately, you need to subdivide each of those tests leading to Grand Prix into process goals because you can control them, you can measure them, and they will get you closer to your product (each level).

One specific example of how to set process goals might be to see what is necessary for your next level test. If the most important element of that test were the extended trot, you might want to see how good you are right now, compare that to how good you need to be, and then set goals, like increasing the extension on your trot so that you can do the diagonal in two fewer strides. Perhaps you need to improve your twenty-meter circles to take that next step. You could, perhaps, set a practice goal to ride well enough so that your coach gives you a thumbs up on your practice circles three times out of four.

You can control the parts that go into conquering a challenge or attaining a goal. That is the benefit of a process goal. It enables you to measure how close you are getting to your end goal. And, if your goals are hopefully realistic, they will be reasonably difficult, but attainable challenges, leading you logically to your destination.

## ROADMAP TO SUCCESS: LEARN FROM THE BEST

Not every discipline has the same organized structure found in dressage. So, how do you find the pieces that make up the goals that will lead to your dream? How do you sort out the skills and drills and experiences you really need versus the ones people just say you need?

One of the best ways to find these pieces and make them mean more to you is by attending the types of events that you dream of participating in or by watching video tapes of those events that interest you to see what success looks like. Go to barns where people are doing the kind of riding you want to do and see what they and their horses do well. You might need to go watch the next level dressage test or witness the skills of top jockeys down the stretch. You might need to see the skills of the Grand Prix horse and rider in the jump off, or the tight turns of the top barrel racers. You might want to watch the style of the top equitation and hunter riders or see what a well-ridden drop looks like in cross-country. Find what you want to do and then watch those people who know how to do it well.

Do this for yourself first. Spend some time watching those riders who do well, and compare them to those who aren't as good. What skill differences can you spot? What seems to be the most important ingredient for success? After a while, you might want to go to an event with a coach, a friend, or someone knowledgeable about you and your skills. Play a game—you tell them first what you think of each ride, and then have them tell you what they think. Do that for every rider (without offending others). You might even want to take a pad of paper and write down those elements you thought made the most difference in each performance.

Before you approach a single coach or ask any advice, think first about the steps you can take on your own to help you get where you want to go. This mental exercise will help you understand both riding and yourself better. After you have jotted down where you are now, where you want to go, and some steps, drills, exercises, or competitions you think will help you on your way, then approach people who have done what you want to do, to see how they did it or how they would do it.

You will find that every time you do this exercise for every new goal, you will become more and more your own coach. Eventually you will get to a stage where you will know better than anyone else exactly what you need to do. Then you will be your own coach.

Jeff Teter discusses a training technique he has used to help other riders improve their skills, get over past mistakes, and learn to be their own coaches.

> "I think the nicest thing that's come about since I've been riding, the last 14 years, is that they've started having cameras at every race meet. You watch the film two or three times and try to have them [riders] explain to you how they thought they rode the race, and then go over it and give your opinion and scenario of what [you] see and what [you] think they can improve on.
>
> "I think the best thing is you let them tell you how they think they rode and what they think they did and what they should do and shouldn't do, and then go over and watch the race and then I give them my scenario, an explanation of what I see and what I think can be improved upon and what [they] should have done and what [they] shouldn't do and go from there."
>
> ~ Jeff Teter

Do not be afraid to approach riders or trainers who are really good, and ask them what skills, exercises, or competitions helped them on their way. As Leslie Webb notes, "The other thing that comes with the maturity of being a wiser and older horseman is that, the older you get the more you're not afraid to ask for help."

*Leslie Webb explains that maturity has made her more willing to seek help from others when she needs it.*

Remember that all the great riders started somewhere. Many of them did not have talent when they started. Great hunter/jumper/rider/coach and United States Equestrian Team coach George Morris has recounted a number of times that his first lesson ended with the instructor advising him to find another sport!

Even those riders who did have talent when they started had only a foot in the door. They had to work at their dreams. Because of this, they will appreciate others who show the same interest, tenacity, and vision as they had. You will be amazed at how interested top riders are at helping you out.

All of these great riders had plans, mental or written, to get where they wanted to go. They all took logical steps to set their goals and move toward their dreams. The defining feature in all of their plans was not any particular drill or any particular technique or style. It was a commitment to get up every morning and put the plan into action, a love for what they were doing, a sense of control over their destiny, and a willingness to experiment.

Any good plan is built on a realistic starting point and some way of assessing progress. You need to do some searching within yourself to determine where you are right now and what you need to do to get to your dream. Remember that people are often poor judges of themselves. You may need help from others to point out what skills and interests you seem to have, and what challenges you *really* face.

You also need to be aware of how far you have come. If you are not making progress, is the plan flawed? Is the effort there? Is there a better way?  Is it focused on the controllable elements, the process pieces?

Direction is the linchpin to happiness and to safety. Once you have your bearings, the challenges are less frightening, because *they make sense.*

## CHAPTER 10

# GETTING THE EXPERIENCE
# WITHOUT THE FEAR

*If everybody would learn to ride, they could ride anything. But they can't ride anything before they learn to ride.*

— Martha Josey

Great riders are rational, thinking people. They know who they are and where they want to go, and they try their best to find ways to get there. If they can't, then they get help from someone else. They use every situation, especially the tough and the uncomfortable ones, as learning experiences. They take their failures and fears apart and reveal them to be made of many conquerable pieces.

Because great riders are well motivated, they often take large rational risks to get them where they want to go. In contrast, people who are confused about what they want out of riding and/or how to achieve their goals often take enormous irrational risks. That is why riders, especially beginners, need good, knowledgeable, and trustworthy people around them to teach them how to take the right steps, to keep those steps from getting too big, and to make sure those steps are in the right direction.

## GOOD INSTRUCTORS CULTIVATE TRUST, MINIMIZE FEAR

Judy Richter, former AHSA Horseman of the Year, and rider and instructor in show-jumping, equitation, and hunters for more than thirty years, explained that trust is the engine of the learning machine because it promotes an enjoyable, safe, and successful learning relationship.

> "Trust is a key to riding instruction. To ensure that learning occurs, the rider must trust her horse, her instructor, and herself. To a great extent, well-placed trust will take care of physical fear. Trust is the product of knowing that you have selected the right instructor, as well as trusting your horse's good instincts, i.e., his basic instinct not to fall or to step on something living."
>
> ~ Judy Richter

Rodney Jenkins maintains this same philosophy about trust.

> "If you have confidence in the people you are working with, that overcomes a lot of fears. Even the people who are taking care of the horses...you have to have a good rapport with them. There's so many variables in there that makes it work."
>
> ~ Rodney Jenkins

That trust, coupled with good teachers, can help riders develop an attitude of hopeful realism, a sense of how to be safe and confident. It will allow them to develop a good sense of how far to stretch themselves. Riders need to learn from people who understand the sport. People who can help set out plans or goals that build upon each other in a series of small controlled risks or sensible chances.

Below, Leslie Webb discusses the feelings of trust placed in her coach, Erich Bubell.

> "I think that you really have to trust yourself. I also

think that there were many times when I was breaking
young horses . . . when they're young, they pull all sorts
of things. My coach was sitting there telling me what
to do and I had to believe in him. If I hadn't, I probably would have jumped off and bailed and said, 'I can't
do this,' but I had to believe in him. Now that he's not
with me [he passed away in 1994], I still need to trust
myself and my instincts."

~ Leslie Webb

Trainer, rider, and author Cherry Hill suggests a method for
achieving a safe and hopefully realistic outlook during practice.

"Your training at home should break each task down
into small, achievable goals. You can divide each obsta-
cle into its component parts [and] master each subgoal."

~ Cherry Hill

By going one step at a time, riders get the chance to feel a
sense of mastery, learn the actual skill, and encounter only small
mental and physical risks at each step.

Knowledgeable trainers like Lavell, Webb, and Hill can help
riders develop their confidence when learning by preventing a
fearful environment to exist. They accomplish this by:

- Developing trust
- Reducing risk
- Maximizing success.

Hill suggests that riders seek "highly competent, savvy
instructors," and suggests "taking time to select an instructor
who is appropriate for your goals, needs, and personality. Then,
listen to that person's advice."

Those instructors will help you combat fear not only by
teaching you the requisite skills and strategies, but also by
encouraging you to take healthy risks on the way to your goals.

When jockey Jeff Teter looked back on his 14 years in racing and on his success and the healthy attitude he's developed

about the sport, he's quick to give credit to steeplechase trainer Janet Elliot (1991 National Steeplechase Association Trainer of the Year), saying she was the prime reason for his great experiences in the sport. Her advice was a key element in his learning experiences.

> "I really attribute my success as much as anything to Janet. Obviously to me she is a tremendous horsewoman for one thing, and she's also a very good teacher. She is very patient. When I was starting out and was making mistakes, she'd sit down and discuss what I was doing, what I should try to do, and was very critical schooling. I mean, that is where you learn as much as anything."
>
> ~ Jeff Teter

Teter points out that the kinds of mistakes beginning unsupervised riders often make, and that he himself made when he first started, can create a poor learning environment with risks of injury and fear of failing.

> "Unfortunately, I see a lot of young riders getting on bad horses and falling right and left. Some may call it fear, or maybe it's smarts, but eventually it's going to get to you . . . and you'll say, 'We ought to look for something else we can do and have fun at,' or you can say, 'I can learn from a couple of falls and try to prevent these things from happening.' A lot of fear has to do with that.

> "When I started . . . the first four races I rode . . . I fell twice and went off-course once. I finished on only one horse. I tried to learn from those mistakes. At the end of that bad day Jonathan Cushman [4-time National Steeple-chase Association Rider of the Year] took me under his wing and he took me aside and said, 'Listen, a lot of these problems you've been having might not

be so much what you are doing. It may have more to do with the horses you're choosing.' "

~ Jeff Teter

Teter is adamant about the importance of good experiences in the learning process to help build confidence, reduce any irrational risks, and keep the game as safe as possible.

"To me it behooves the trainer who has a young or green rider to put them in the position to get a good learning experience right from their first ride rather than putting them on something that basically is a major risk. I think the worst scenario you can possibly have is to have a green rider and a green horse."

"The biggest thing is to surround yourself with knowledgeable people such as trainers who have the best interest for you, like what happened with me."

~ Jeff Teter

## THE HORSE–RIDER RELATIONSHIP

Carol Lavell has chosen not to remain in training with difficult horses, and, as an instructor, she often suggests the same thing to her students. She has decided that those kinds of risks do not add to the direction she is going in riding, and therefore are irrational. She is not afraid to get help from others in her quest for the best experience.

"Breaking these young horses is extremely difficult and they can really hurt you. Now I start my young ones on the lunge and if I see that there's a problem coming, I send them right down the road to a jumper rider in whose shoes I was 20 years ago. He works on them and they run away with him or they buck him off or they rear and fall over backwards on the lunge with him. Then, when that's all over he sends them back as being good, ... or he says ... 'You know, this one has a marble loose. It would be a better idea if you sent this one down the road.' And if that's the case ... I do that. So I've gotten smart in that direction.

"Also, now I step forward with a sure sense of ethics with riders with a problem horse. Now instead of just pushing the riders and saying, 'We can deal with this problem,' or, 'I'll try my very best to deal with this problem,' now I say, 'Nope. I like you a whole lot better than I like this horse. There are 6 million horses in the United States and who has to ride this one? Why bother with this one?' "

~ Carol Lavell

Lavell says that the horses her students ride and their level of comfort or discomfort with their horses is her primary safety guide. She also explains that the logic of getting riders on the best possible, safest horse to learn seems so obvious to her ... but finds it frustrating that it sometimes eludes her students.

"Any person who is afraid of her horse is impossible to teach. You have to compromise so much on what we want done with the horse. I have to bank on the fact that the horse himself will get better trained without confronting any issues and without confronting the rider and her fear. The rider might not be able to address the horse's problem, and if we did pursue that route I might get the rider hurt. And then there is the possibility that the rider will not ride either [due to the bad experience]. There are all kinds of possibilities along this scale, from a dead rider to one who says I won't ride anymore.

"I come with a lot of credentials so I carry a little clout when I tell people that I would prefer they get off a horse ... when I say that this horse has a problem that is very difficult to get rid of, especially in a mature horse . . . that this kind of horse is going to hurt you. I find a lot of these riders, even with the clout that I have, say, 'Well, it's the only horse I've got and I don't know what else I'm going to do except try to deal with her problem.' They just don't listen."

~ Carol Lavell

Martha Josey says that her school in Texas keeps in mind some of those same key points for preventing fear.

"Horses are dangerous, and people can get hurt. We teach that all the time. I think with most people what happens is they got on that one horse and they were scared. It scared the horse, and the horse ran off and they had that bad experience. I would never . . . put a beginner or somebody who was scared on a horse that was going to run off with them. So, what a person needs to always remember is to start out and be under-mounted in the beginning."

~ Martha Josey

As for her own experiences learning, Josey explains that she had gradual training, and that, due to this type of gradual learning process, she now felt she had few limitations, that she can "ride anything" at this point. She stated that, "If everybody would learn to ride, they could ride anything. But they can't ride anything before they learn to ride."

"When I was a little girl I started out on a little pony, which was wonderful. My dad was one of the first directors of the National Quarter Horse Association, so he certainly knew the kind of horses to put me on. And I graduated into better horses all along."

~ Martha Josey

Rodney Jenkins believes that a trusting horse-rider relationship is important for gaining mileage and confidence, especially with a nervous rider.

> "I really think what happens to so many riders is that they don't pick the best horse. You've got to have a horse that suits you. You know you want the super horse, but maybe the super horse doesn't suit you.

> "I'd rather have a horse for a nervous rider that's an old Grand Prix four-faulter. They might have four faults every ride, but if they get around that ring, sooner or later they [the students] are going to learn to ride that horse and they are going to get better and better. But if you put them on a super careful horse, and they make that same mistake, that horse usually is going to slam them because he'll stop. The most careful horses will stop, because they don't want to get hurt. So if you get a nervous rider and a nervous horse that is careful, you get a hell of a scene on your hands. All of a sudden you've got a horse that is not going to accomplish what he could, and you've got a rider that's going to be afraid to try to accomplish [goals]."
>
> ~ Rodney Jenkins

Jenkins also explains that choosing the right person to help you find a horse is important, and that actually selecting the horse is a critical process.

> "I say you need to look for somebody who can help you pick that horse. Somebody you trust. Somebody who knows what you're looking for, and you have to believe in them. There are so many people who will just take the word of somebody they don't really know.

> "Also, you can't tell about a horse by just looking at it either. You ride it and that's the only way you know. I've seen a million horses jump great when I'm watch-

ing, but when *I* ride them they've horrified me.

"If you don't like that horse when you try him, even though he jumps great, don't buy him. You'll always have this mental block from then on of, 'I didn't really like him when I bought him, but he jumped so good.' Well there's a million reasons he might have jumped good that day."

~ Rodney Jenkins

## THE PROPER LEARNING ENVIRONMENT

As an instructor, Jenkins works carefully, especially with a timid rider, to make sure there is a good, mentally safe learning environment.

"You just try to get them relaxed, and tell them how great they are doing. You can't ever tear a person like that down because they already over-try. They are over-achievers, so the more you get after them, the more they get wrong. They always think about quitting.

"You always try to give them confidence. A very nervous person is like a nervous horse. The more confidence you give them the better they do.

"I've seen kids walk out of the ring, and people will jump on them like the plague. And those kids already know what they did wrong. When you do that, all you are doing is embarrassing some young person or some older person, and making them look like an idiot in front of people.

"There is no point to being that negative. If you are going to be negative . . . wait until you get back to that barn. Let them cool off and be a little upset. When they settle down and you can kind of go over that thing with them, then when they leave there, nobody has known that you said anything to them except them. Otherwise, the rider will be like, 'Oh God, am I this awful that I should be humiliated?' "

~ Rodney Jenkins

Judy Richter believes that "One of the most crucial tasks of a responsible riding instructor is to prevent fear in riders." Her three steps are to:

" . . . not overmount the rider . . . not overface the rider . . . [and use] good preventive techniques such as learning in advance how to cope with bolting or bucking and carefully planned exercises such as a clear routine or pattern."

~ Judy Richter

When Jeff Teter was a beginner, he often had difficulty understanding his trainer. He did not understand Elliot's rationale for allowing him to ride only certain horses. In both the case of Lavell's students and the case of Teter's training, it was hard for trainees to understand what risks were best not taken (at least yet). Teter said:

"You can ask Janet, we did get into discussions. I felt that when I started riding for Janet sort of fairly regularly, that there were still certain horses in the barn that I still wasn't allowed to ride in a race. I'd say, 'How come I can ride this one, this one, and this one, but you won't let me ride this one?' But she always had good explanations."

~ Jeff Teter

Teter believes that one of the reasons a great learning environment is so important for any rider is that getting a bad start, injury-wise or failure-wise, makes it tougher to get back on track down the road. Even though we have a choice over what we think, having experienced numerous failures and/or injuries can lead to some bad thinking habits that, like any habit, are hard to break. People can get used to seeing things in a negative light all the time and thinking bad thoughts. That causes a cycle of irrational thoughts and bad performances or injuries that continue to feed a negative self-fulfilling spiral of injuries and/or self-doubt.

> "Positives build on positives, and negatives build on negatives. The most critical thing is building confidence when you are a young jockey. The smart trainer sees this pattern and really thinks about how to get that effect. I think the biggest thing is the experience. The key to this sport is the first two, three, five years of getting to know the horses and getting confidence in yourself and avoiding the negative experience to put doubt in your mind. I was fortunate enough to not get hurt too badly."
>
> ~ Jeff Teter

Teter goes on to explain about some of the things that happen to people who harbor fears. "If fear is in the back of your mind," he says, "It starts to affect your riding. I've seen people who are on a horse that they feel will be tough for them, and they'll start to hold back." He adds that part of the problem is that the fear keeps them from riding correctly.

> "You're going to jeopardize yourself, because you're a little lax or a little hesitant about doing something. I think you put yourself, if not everybody else [in the race], at risk because, all of a sudden, you are a split second behind what your normal reactions would be had you not been scared."
>
> ~ Jeff Teter

Leslie Webb suggests that setting safety standards, reasonable goals, and a reasonable pace of learning were the best ways to get her students to where they wanted to go while preventing and combating fear.

"I have a lot of students who . . . are completely afraid of their horse. Which is to me absolutely amazing that they love to ride, because they are scared to death of it.

"It's kind of a high for them and all that, but what I've learned through the years of teaching is that what I have to do is to teach them to be safe. What I decided is that we have to be safe number one. In their own realm [level of comfort], whatever feels safe, we work with them. And they succeed that way. It comes in little itty bitty steps. From that point of view, for this particular person, I pat myself on the back and say 'Listen, we've done a great job.' Maybe it took two years rather than six months, or whatever . . . there are just so many scenarios like that. You just have to take your time."

~ Leslie Webb

## CHAPTER 11

# SOME PRACTICAL TIPS

*Learn to think like your horse. Understand that he fears liverpools [water jumps] and that he always knows where "home" or the ingate is. This will assist greatly in anticipating your horse's behavior.*
~ Judy Richter

W hile this is not a book on riding safety, it is good to keep in mind some practical tips to reduce dangerous situations that can come up during riding.

**A SIMPLE GUIDE TO SAFER RIDES**
Judy Richter suggests three guidelines for any coach seeking to promote safe riding. First:

> "Do not overmount the rider, either in terms of the horse's temperament or his size. There are individual differences in what scares people about riding, as well as what makes them feel more comfortable. If the rider fears the height or temperament of a particular horse, move back to a mount that is within the individual's comfort range until confidence begins to build. A rider's comfort or discomfort may also emanate from the conformation of a particular horse, e.g., "downhill" horses whose forward slant may make the rider feel as if she is pitching forward off the front of the horse."
> ~ Judy Richter

Virtually every rider we spoke to mentioned the importance of having a good horse-rider match. Jeff Teter and Leslie Webb both expressed that their careers had been good enough that neither one went out of their way to get on tough horses; Greg Ryan talked about selecting horses carefully and using risk management; Valerie Kanavy and Carol Lavell pointed out that there are a million other horses in the world . . . so not to dwell on a bad one; Rodney Jenkins talked about finding a horse that really suited you best; and, Martha Josey talked about starting out on an easy horse.

It is a virtual consensus that there is no learning advantage to riding a horse that does not suit you. Riding difficult horses will only help teach you how to deal with difficult horses. If that is your goal, fine, but if not . . . why risk it?

Richter's second rule is about being a hopeful realist, and finding the right level of stretching without having any tearing.

> "Do not overface the rider. Here, a balance is necessary between backing up to easier exercises when the rider is fearful, and encouraging the rider to stretch him or herself as much as possible. The instructor must judge carefully how to bring the rider's skills forward without pushing too far, into the realm of fear."
>
> ~ Judy Richter

John Lyons has a system for achieving just that effect. He suggests two rules to make a sensible progression of tasks without creating fear.

> "Break tasks down into smaller, easier pieces, to help ensure a "success experience" that will build the rider's confidence and sense of control. This may mean removing the horse completely from initial exercises, or beginning with leading the horse from the ground. If mounted, it may consist of just getting on and off the horse, or simply riding at a walk in a small pen.

"Move ahead to more advanced work only when the
rider is bored with the exercise. This ensures that the
rider will not be pushed beyond his/her limit, and will
begin to sense control before a new task is attempted."
                                                    ~ John Lyons

Richter's third rule suggests preparation as a key, something
that Lyons wholly agrees with. He says that exercises are more
clear and predictable (and thus less fear inducing) if you, "Set
specific patterns for the rider to follow."

" . . . good preventive techniques such as learning in
advance how to cope with bolting or bucking and carefully planned exercises such as a clear routine of patterns to be practiced can help . . . "
                                                    ~ Judy Richter

Preparation is the key to reducing risks and reducing any
fear of injury, just as preparing for a competition by practicing
the right skills can reduce your fear of failure. Preparation as a
coach or rider should consist of preparing for the best and the
worst and using every good and bad experience along the way as
a teaching or learning tool. Every mistake is a step closer to success, if used properly. Learn from the error, be it failure or
falling, but get rid of the sting.

"All of that [maturity] comes with time, and doing the
sport, and overcoming and learning to 'eat' the bad
days. Learn something from the bad days but for God's
sake don't eat them for breakfast. You can't eat it for
breakfast because if you do, you're going to be worse
the next day. Go somewhere and get it over with. Get
up the next morning and ride. Do what you do best.
Don't bring your garbage and baggage with you because
it just eats at you."
                                                    ~ Rodney Jenkins

Webb believes that learning from mistakes, fixing them, and keeping track of this process is vital to learning. This applies not only to skill mistakes but also to dangerous or injurious mistakes as well. As a rider, you should remember your mistakes, learn from them, but discard the sting.

> "I think that they just have to take each day's lesson, each day they ride, and kind of put a little mental note in, 'I know this happened today, and how did I fix it.' I think that's probably the one thing that separates the amateurs from the professionals—they [amateurs] tend to forget."
>
> ~ Leslie Webb

Jeff Teter agrees:

> "Learn from what you did wrong and try to turn that into a positive for the next time. Learn from that . . . [and] . . . hopefully when that same scenario comes up again you won't do the same thing because it is apt to be unsuccessful again. If you don't learn, then obviously you're not going to be successful."
>
> ~ Jeff Teter

Other elements of the environment that should be controlled include the safety of the riding arena (holes, sharp objects, low ceilings, etc.) and the noise level (avoid areas where there will be sudden, unexpected noise). If there are problems with any of these aspects of the riding environment, then the learning process will be threatened, and danger increased.

Other potential problems include coaches, other riders, parents, and spectators. For example, a coach may use training equipment improperly or arrange the ring or training aids, such as jumps, poorly during practice. Riders who do not keep adequate spacing between their horses can pose problems as can parents who insist their children be pushed to unrealistic levels, or who disturb practices by their presence. Finally, spectators who are loud, throw things, or who take attention away from important safety cues, such as the instructor's warnings about any obstacles in the way, or the horse's mood, can create problems.

## A RIDER'S PERSONAL RESPONSIBILITY

All the elements that go into creating a proper learning environment serve to make your riding experience a success. However, it is your own responsibility to question those challenges that include risks you do not want to take. You must pay attention to things that contribute to your sense of ease and safety, and avoid those that detract from it. Remember, you need to take good risks to grow, and avoid the bad ones that could get you seriously injured.

## EQUIPMENT

One special element of personal responsibility is properly maintaining your equipment. Being cheap about replacing your worn stirrup leathers will be hard to justify from a hospital bed. Many riders are concerned about their appearance and will not wear helmets. You must remember that you are more likely to be seriously injured or killed without one. We will not preach. Your life is your responsibility.

Many barns in the race business now insist that their riders wear slam vests, or flak jackets commonly seen on eventers or in steeplechasing. This is an additional, "uncool looking" safety option that has saved many lives. If you feel self-conscious about wearing either the helmet or the jacket, just remember that seat belts were considered a joke just 15 years ago and now routinely save lives. Airbags were also considered a joke just five years ago, but have also saved lives. Do what you will, but remember, not having safe equipment is voluntarily accepting more risk that offers no corresponding benefit to your training.

Judy Richter suggests the following advice for the rider who wants to take responsibility for a safe learning experience.

• "First, focus on prevention. Analyze the realities of the situation, whether it is a jumping course or [some other] exercise, and be certain that all possible safety measures are in place. This will not only lessen the probabilities of an accident, but will give you, the rider, an added sense of security.

• "If you begin to experience fear, back up a bit to some simplified work. Fear may mean that you are pushing beyond your comfortable limit, or your limit on a particular mount.

• "Try not to overdo 'analysis,' particularly of errors. Instead, figure out what can be done without dwelling on negatives. For performance anxiety, focus on various parts of the course to be ridden, but in an effort to work through them rather than catastrophize about them. Also, step back to easier classes, where it is easier to be more laid-back about your performance.

• "There is a danger in being 'too careful.' While I certainly do not recommend being rash, there is a point at which the rider must let go, must let things happen rather than insist on making them happen. Sometimes misjudgments occur, and must be lived, or ridden, through.

• "Learn to think like your horse. Understand that he fears liverpools [water jumps] and that he always knows where 'home' or the in-gate is. This will assist greatly in anticipating your horse's behavior.

• "Remember that the horse and rider are a team. Take all preventive measures that are possible for both horse and rider—then stop fearing neurotically about the horse's safety. What I mean here is that once you have done all that is possible to ensure a safe ride, give up catastrophic thinking about your horse, not only about yourself.

• "Know yourself. Be realistic about what you can do, what you are capable of achieving. Stretch to achieve the best riding of which you are capable, but keep a keen and realistic eye on what the ceiling of your abilities is."

~ Judy Richter

We often feel that difficult horses are simply dangerous. A trusted expert needs to play a part in any decision to work with such an animal. Understand that people often stick with what is comfortable and familiar, even when they know it is dangerous, in an effort to avoid the discomfort of change. If your horse is getting in the way of your mission in riding, you may need to make some painful decisions that will save you grief later. Remember, as Lavell said, "With problem horses, I say cut and run. *Cut and run.* How much you lose here is only your own personal gain."

## CHAPTER 12

# YOU HOLD THE REINS

*Learn from what you did wrong and try to turn that into a positive for the next time. If you don't learn, then obviously you're not going to be successful.*

~ Jeff Teter

Most people are not even aware of the rapid and often flawed way that they think, whether interpreting nervous energy or sizing up a given situation. We hope we've helped you see that while people often have a terribly flawed view of reality, they also have control over their thoughts and actions. Decisions about the size of a risk, how much ability you have to handle it, and, finally, whether to give it a try, are all subject to interpretation.

## SOME ENCOURAGEMENTS FOR RATIONAL THINKING: FREE WILL

In the end, you are still the master of your own fate. You can choose to do or not do those things you fear. You can take off your skewed glasses, be a realist, and find a way to succeed with what you have. Or, you can give in to comfort and choose to stick to your own irrational, habitual views of yourself. It is that simple. If you want something badly, yet will not help yourself to find a way to do it, you are selling yourself short. You have free will and are personally responsible for the direction you choose, both in riding and in life.

You may be frightened and you may have had bad experiences in the past, but a rational person will find a way to do what they want to do. If it is difficult, so be it. Life is not easy, and we all have our own weaknesses and fears, but it is our choice whether we give in to them and give up on our hopes.

As we have said many times, people are often poor evaluators of their own abilities, and of the magnitude of the challenges ahead of them. Chances are your fears are founded partially on reality and partially on fiction. You need to:

- Pare down your fears to a logical core.

- Determine what you need to do to beat your fear and get where you are headed.

- Live on the edge and assume that you can succeed.

- See how someone like you might go about accomplishing this task.

- Be active in life, not passive.

- Question the stream of mental garbage that treats you badly and fight it with every ounce of your being.

- Be a hopeful realist. See what you really have going for you and then find a solution that someone with your skills can achieve.

- Do not hurt yourself by giving in to your own skewed thinking, or by taking on something you cannot do . . . be a realist and start looking for solutions.

- Don't start downing yourself. Give yourself a run for your money. Play devil's advocate. For every reason you give yourself about why you can't do something you want to do, find two strategies that will help get you there. Remember, you have to sell yourself on you, and that's the hardest thing in the world to do.

Developing rational thinking is like keeping a clean bed-room—lack of constant attention leads to disorder. When you want a clean room, you don't throw your clothes on the floor. That would be irrational. Likewise, if you want something badly, yet spend day and night looking for reasons why you will fail or get hurt doing that thing, then you are being irrational. If you want something badly enough, you must be willing to fight your own tendency to stand in your own way.

Successful riders find excuses to succeed. They know better than anyone what they can and cannot do and they work with that. Rodney Jenkins was not comfortable taking the risk of using speed in jump-offs, so he used turns to win more Grand Prix in the U.S. than any other rider. Jeff Teter and Greg Ryan were also uncomfortable going at top speed until the last fence, and Teter said he wouldn't even go all out at the last, and they both had incredible records. Carol Lavell and Valerie Kanavy knew that problem horses were not their cup of tea, and they are medalists. Leslie Webb, Greg Best, and Valerie Kanavy all had trouble with nerves, but they developed strategies to combat them and won medals. The list could go on.

All of these riders found ways around their limitations. Ones they could win with. As Carol Lavell says, the name of the game is to play up the things you know how to do and work on the other areas during practice if you need to.

> "I start them off and say, 'You know I want you to go to as many schooling shows as possible' . . . and when they are warming up in the warm-up ring and they are going, 'Oh, see he's doing this again. I just can't get this right.' I say, 'He didn't get that right last week or the week before that and he's not going to get it right next month either. That part's wrong . . . so leave that alone . . . He'll do that wrong in the ring and at least you can count on doing that wrong in the ring. Just fudge through that and go on to the things he can do. We are

going to compete just to show some of the things
that we do well and to see where the horse is in his
training.' "

~ Carol Lavell

If you want to conquer your fears, nothing succeeds like
success. Every time you conquer a fear you will feel incredible.
Plan and prepare mentally and physically, but most of all, go out
there and get some wise guidance to help you start taking sensible risks toward your goals. Overcoming your fear is going to
mean attacking skewed  thinking and proving to yourself, both
in thought and in action, that you can do it. It takes being tenacious to succeed, says Ryan.

> "Being tenacious is more important than being talent-
> ed. A tenacious person is going to have setbacks. If he's
> not as talented, he's going to have setbacks. He's going
> to have to learn to deal with failure, and he's going to
> have to learn to deal with fear. And when he does final-
> ly accomplish his goal, well, to him, it will be so much
> more rewarding than for the talented person."
>
> ~ Greg Ryan

It is easy to drift with the current of your own thoughts,
and accept your own confused reality, because it is a well-prac-
ticed habit. Take a chance and look at how you are thinking
about yourself . . . especially when you feel fear. Judy Richter says
it is most important to:

> " . . . know yourself. Be realistic about what you can do,
> what you are capable of achieving. Stretch to achieve
> the best riding of which you are capable, but keep a
> keen and realistic eye on what the ceiling of your ability
> is."
>
> ~ Judy Richter

The idea is to be a hopeful realist. One who knows the reality of the present situation, but is always looking for ways to improve or get closer to some goal at every opportunity. This is expressed in healthy experimentation to stretch your own mental and physical limits, as well as by seeking new information for yourself and for your horse. Valerie Kanavy talks about this process in her life.

> "I'm not searching for a guru, but I think that it's kind of important to always keep an open mind and evaluate some new information. You have to trust in yourself too, but you have to have an open mind. There is always information that you haven't thought of, or a different perspective in handling or addressing a training technique or a problem, that you know you can use."
>
> ~ Valerie Kanavy

That stretch to make progress includes taking reasonable risks of failure, looking and feeling stupid, and getting injured. We have shown you how hopeful realism is the advantage that top riders have, and we have shown you how they got it, and how you can get it too.

Enjoy every risk you take, and take healthy risks of failure often. Be the safest rider you can be, while headed on your way to your dreams. Do not listen to yourself or others when they get in your way. Be an experimenter. See how far you can go, and use this secret wisely. Remember, fear and excitement are two horns on the same bull.

# APPENDIX

---

# FACING DIFFERENT FEARS

## PERSONAL CASE STUDIES

# FACING DIFFERENT FEARS

Conquering fear can begin when you decide where you want to go, and assess whether the thing you fear is a necessity to that journey. Any fear, either rational or irrational, can prevent you from doing something that you really need to do to succeed. We will show you some ways to get past those fears. Below is a simple plan to follow with any fear. After that we will present a number of case studies, and the key elements to overcome them.

## THE GOAL: WHY DO THIS THING?

The first thing you need to do when facing a fearful situation is decide whether it fits into your goals. Why bother learning to overcome a fear that has nothing to do with the direction you want to go in riding? If you have always dreamed of being a steeplechase jockey, you will need to learn to deal with jumping at speed and the fact that there is some danger involved. If that scares you, then you will need to learn to handle that fear so that you can jump at speed. Giving up on the thing you want so badly would be irrational. If you have always dreamed of being a national class dressage rider, then jumping at speed is not likely to be a goal that will help you to your dream. In that case fear can be rational because it prevents you from doing something that might be dangerous that you don't need to do.

Every time you fear something you should decide whether it fits into where you are going. If it does fit in, then you should search high and low for the best ways to overcome it. The ways to overcome it are both mental (thought-stopping, disputation, imagery) and physical (doing).

In all the examples we will explore below, there are two possible responses. One is to recognize that the thing you fear is *not* something that you need to do to get to where you want to go. In that case, there is *no point* trying to take on that challenge. It may pose unacceptable risks for you and actually hurt your chances of going where you want to go (especially if it causes you to be injured or to lose confidence). One response that is always available is to decide that the challenge is not worthwhile. The other response is to decide that it is a worthwhile challenge.

Only one response, *overcoming a rational challenge*, is presented here. We are *not* implying that everyone should take on every challenge. What we *are* doing is showing how, once you have decided that you want to do something you fear, you might choose to do it.

### 1. ADMIT THAT YOU ARE AFRAID

You need to admit to yourself with great honesty that you are afraid. Sometimes this is difficult, but it is a part of the process. You cannot help yourself combat fear if you cannot admit to yourself that you have any fear.

### 2. DISCOVER WHY YOU ARE AFRAID (IF YOU CAN)

Remember that time last year when your friend's horse ran away with her and she was nearly killed. Ask yourself honestly whether you've thought very much about that incident. If you discover that you do indeed think about that event very regularly, and most often when preparing to ride or actually riding, then you should realize that this memory, along with irrational self-talk, is triggering fearful responses in your own riding experience.

Perhaps it is not that simple. You may never have experienced a brush with injury, or know anyone else who is fearful. It is often easier to identify fears if you can relate them to actual bad experiences. But some irrational fears can arise out of any number of less obvious sources, and it is more complicated to discover their origins.

### 3. DECIDE THAT YOU NEED TO DO THIS THING TO GET WHERE YOU WANT TO GO

As we noted above, and throughout the book, especially in Chapter 4, "Good Risks vs Bad Risks: Facing Fear as a Matter of Personal Goals," the things you should and should not face are entirely up to your impression of where you are going, and how you want to get there. It is a very personal decision.

### 4. IDENTIFY HOW YOU KNOW YOU ARE AFRAID

This sounds like an odd step, but it is crucial to understanding the fear. Do you know you are afraid because you can *feel adrenaline* running through you? Does the feeling scare you? Do you feel afraid because you have identified irrational *self-talk* that you have about the challenge before you? Are you having *self-defeating conversations* with yourself? Is the fear coming from *images of disaster* associated with tackling the challenge? Pay attention to the things you are telling yourself, the images you are creating in your mind, and the way you feel.

### 5. USE MENTAL PRACTICE TO HELP PREPARE YOUR MIND AND BODY

Mentally run through the challenge as if you were actually there. Use this first mental run-through to examine the thoughts and feelings you usually have when taking on a difficult challenge that you fear. Use the mental imagery skills that we discussed in the section "Mental Imagery: The Mind and Body," in Chapter 7. Find a quiet place and create a mental picture of the situation that you fear. Use all your senses to make the crispest possible image of the fearful situation. Put yourself in the saddle and imagine every element of how you feel—the tingles of adrenaline and the way you usually think when facing the situation. Picture all of the relevant information regarding the task . . . the size of the jump or the number of people in the crowd, or the amount of pressure you feel.

Take the situation apart and break it into smaller pieces.

Picture yourself facing a smaller version of the challenge you fear, and then gradually increase the size of it after each successful run-through until it is the size of the actual challenge. If you fear the pressure of competition, then imagine competing in a small competition. Mentally practice your routine several times gradually increasing the size of the competition and the importance of the event in your mind after each successful mental run-through. If the size of a fence is the problem, imagine jumping small fences first, and then larger and larger ones after each successful run-through until you reach the size you fear—and then master it mentally. Imagine the sights, smells, sensations, and sounds to make it as real as possible. Be particularly sure to imagine the thing you fear as accurately as possible. Imagery builds confidence and also actually exercises neurons in the brain and nerves in the body to give the mind and the body *actual practice as well.*

### 6. USE PHYSICAL PRACTICE TO HELP PREPARE YOUR MIND AND BODY

Just as with the mental imagery . . . be aware of your thoughts and images at each stage of the game. Take the challenge apart into smaller pieces and take them on one by one. Keep everything small and simple and take moderate steps of increasing difficulty each time. Nothing succeeds like success, so make yourself take some healthy risks and do the thing that you have always wanted to do. By doing this you will make facing the fear an unconscious habit.

### 7. RECOGNIZE SELF-DEFEATING THOUGHTS (I'M NO GOOD) AND BEHAVIORS (STOP TRYING), STOP THEM, DISPUTE THE FAULTY LOGIC BEHIND THEM, AND REPLACE THEM WITH APPROPRIATE (RATIONAL) THOUGHTS

Think about the way that you know that you are afraid, and the information on your thoughts and images you have gathered from actual experiences. What do you say to yourself in these fearful situations? Anytime, in mental practice or actual practice or in competition, that you hear something that is negative and is *interfering* with what you want to do:

    A. Recognize it,

    B. Stop beating yourself up with it,

    C. Dispute the irrational aspects of it,

    D. Replace it with something rational and constructive.

Once you can hear the negative thought (recognize it), then find a reason why the negative thought is flawed. For example a rider might have the thought, "I can't ride in front of all these people. I'll make a fool out of myself and that would be terrible." First identify that the thought is not helpful. It will not add to her performance. As a rider she should say, "I can see that thinking this way makes me feel I can't do this and that it makes me feel fear." Now that she knows that this thought is not helpful, she can use disputing or, if time is of the essence, first she can use thought-stopping (see Chapter 3). She can destroy the thought by interrupting it in her mind by saying, "STOP, NO, NO, NO!" She can also picture the negative thought as a target that she can destroy, "BANG!"

Time permitting, she can *dispute* the thought she had, and replace it with a new and better one. She could look for the flawed logic in the negative thoughts by saying, "I have practiced for many months for this show and I want to do well, so thinking bad thoughts is just going to hurt me. I can see that I'm thinking irrationally because my thoughts are keeping me from doing what I want to do—I want to place at this show. I am only human, and while it is true that I might mess up *even though* I practiced a lot, I'm the one who cares the most, not the crowd. I cannot *demand* perfection from myself any more than I could demand that from anybody else. I can see that I'm holding myself to unreasonable standards of perfection that I would never hold my best friend to. So now I need to be my own best friend. Even the best people mess up."

Now that she has realized that she has been overly demanding of herself, she can develop a new and better thought to

---

### A GENERAL GUIDE TO THINKING RATIONALLY

This is a "quick and dirty" guide of ways to tell if you are thinking rationally (dealing with reality and looking for solutions not problems—HOPEFUL REALISM) or are being irra-

| IRRATIONAL | RATIONAL |
|---|---|
| Awfulizing | Moderate evaluations of how bad things are |
| Intolerant of frustration | Tolerant |
| Overly critical of self and others | Acceptance that all humans make mistakes |
| Absolutists— Things must work. Things should work. | Flexible— Things may work. I prefer if things work. |

---

replace it like, "I'm just going to go out there and show them that we can do the things that we practiced. If I mess up, that's okay because nobody is perfect."

This process works for real situations and for mental imagery as well. In fact, the more times you practice this process mentally, the better you become at doing it in real life, and the fewer times you will think negative thoughts. You will be learning a new habit—thinking well of yourself when facing challenges instead of beating yourself up, being overly demanding, and feeling fear.

# PERSONAL CASE STUDIES

## CASE ONE

**SITUATION.**

Adult beginner who is afraid of horses because they are so big.

**WHY DO THIS?**

Social reasons. She is engaged to be married to a man who rides. Her future in-laws ride together as a family on weekends and holidays. She wants to join them.

**AM I AFRAID?**

"Yes," she admits, "horses are big animals, and I'm concerned I might get hurt."

**DO I KNOW WHY I AM AFRAID?**

"Yes. I fell off a horse as a child and got badly hurt. I haven't felt comfortable around horses since then."

**IS THIS SOMETHING THAT I NEED TO DO?**

"Absolutely," she insists. "I've made the decision to marry this man and I want to take part in the family's main sporting activity. I definitely do not want to be left out of this important family pastime.

**WHAT ARE MY THOUGHTS AND IMAGES WHEN I'M FEARFUL?**

"I see him stepping on me, or turning suddenly and hitting me with his head, or even kicking me. I think, 'I'm going to get killed. I don't know enough to feel safe around any horse.' "

**MENTALLY PRACTICE.**

Begin by imaging the horse you ride, and the situations where you are most fearful. In this example it is a stall approach.

### VIVID AND REAL.

See all the details of the situation. The color of the horse, the barn, the stall, the smell of the shavings or straw. Imagine approaching the horse.

### BREAK INTO PIECES.

See the horse, and the approach in stages. Make the horse as small as a cat, and each time through increase the size. See the approach with each strategy: 1. hand out, 2. touch shoulder, 3. hand on halter.

### PHYSICALLY PRACTICE.

"Well, here it goes . . . I'm in the stall, and sure the horse tried to bite me, but I stood my ground like coach said, and I swatted the horse on the nose. The whole thing made feel a little queasy, but I know it is from the adrenaline. I feel better about myself now."

### DEFEAT IRRATIONAL THOUGHTS AND IMAGES DURING MENTAL AND PHYSICAL PRACTICE.

"I'm too old to learn this stuff. The horses are huge and dangerous, and I cannot picture me ever getting past this. I might as well quit. I can see me getting hurt badly."

### RECOGNIZE.

"I really want to learn to ride. Not a single one of these negative thoughts is going to help me improve."

### STOP.

NO! NO! NO! STOP! BANG!

### DISPUTE.

"I am demanding absolute safety from my riding experience. I know that even the best get hurt. I need to concentrate on the safety, *not* on my fears when I get in the stall."

**REPLACE.**

"I have practiced mentally and physically going in that stall a million times. The more times I do it, the better I will feel. I'm going to go in there and do what I know how to do and if it does not work . . . I'll learn from it."

## CASE TWO

**SITUATION.**

Adult beginner who is afraid of being injured.

**WHY DO THIS?**

This has been a desire for quite some time. She enjoys trail rides and has become addicted to their stress-relieving properties. She wants to keep doing them no matter what.

**AM I AFRAID?**

"I'm afraid that I'm going to get hurt out on the trail. I'm a mother of two, and I support my family . . . so *yes* I'm scared. I'll get hurt!"

**DO I KNOW WHY I AM AFRAID?**

"Yes. My cousin broke her back after being thrown from a horse. She eventually recovered but had to take an extended disability leave from her job and I could never afford to do that."

**IS THIS SOMETHING THAT I NEED TO DO?**

"I get so much enjoyment out of riding (and so much stress relief too) that I would never give it up. I get too much out of it to ever stop doing it."

**WHAT ARE MY THOUGHTS AND IMAGES WHEN I'M FEARFUL?**

"I can see my horse, who is pretty spooky, wheeling (which he has done many times) and dropping me on my head and killing me. I keep thinking that I'm being a terrible mother for putting my family in a position to lose me to injury."

**MENTALLY PRACTICE.**

Begin by imaging the horse you ride, and the situations where you are most fearful. In this example it is a trail ride.

**VIVID AND REAL.**

See all the details of the situation. The wind and the chill in the air. The sudden noise to the left. The snort as the horse stops and prepares to spin.

**BREAK INTO PIECES.**

See the horse, and the approach in stages. Make the horse weak and unable to get away with the wheel . . . and then make it stronger and stronger. Picture your successful response to each piece . . . 1. the stop, 2. the prop, 3. the spin.

**PHYSICALLY PRACTICE.**

Ride the horse with an instructor out on the trail and prepare for the wheel by being relaxed and developing some strategies to prevent and defeat the wheel. Have the instructor assess the horse. Is this horse a problem horse? Is this a problem to be solved, or one to be replaced with another horse?

**DEFEAT IRRATIONAL THOUGHTS AND IMAGES DURING MENTAL AND PHYSICAL PRACTICE.**

"I'm a terrible mother and a terrible rider. I can just see all the damage this horse could do to me, and it wouldn't be hurting just me, I would be hurting my whole family. I must keep this rotten horse because I don't want to be a quitter."

**RECOGNIZE.**

"I can see that all these negative thoughts are ruining any of the fun I used to have riding. I really need to do something about this."

**STOP.**

NO! NO! NO! STOP! BANG!

**DISPUTE.**

"My coach says that this horse is a little rank. I'm not trying to train to be a rodeo rider of any sort . . . I'm being nuts holding on to this rotten horse. The problem is not that I'm a terrible mother or rider . . . the problem is that I spent money on a rotten horse. It's going to be tough to get rid of it, but I must dump him if I want to enjoy the sport."

**REPLACE.**

"I have practiced mentally and physically defeating this problem in the horse, and I now know that I can handle my horse most of the time. But, I'm not enjoying this horse and enjoyment is what I want, so I'm going to get rid of this horse and then the problem (my horse) will be gone and I can enjoy."

## CASE THREE

**SITUATION.**
Adult beginner who is afraid of failing.

**WHY DO THIS?**
"I have been riding for a little while now and I think it is time to see how good I am."

**AM I AFRAID?**
"Yes," she says, "I am afraid that I will let myself down, that I won't be very good."

**DO I KNOW WHY I AM AFRAID?**
"Yes. It is of paramount importance to me personally that I excel at everything I do. (I wouldn't like myself as well if I were mediocre, and I wouldn't expect others to like me either, if I weren't so excellent at my endeavors.) Riding is my newest challenge."

**IS THIS SOMETHING THAT I NEED TO DO?**
"I really want to see if I have improved, and this is what I want to become good at (competing), so I really want to do it."

**WHAT ARE MY THOUGHTS AND IMAGES WHEN I'M FEARFUL?**
"I see me losing my stirrup and then fumbling around trying to get it back, or sometimes I see myself stepping out of the dressage ring and getting disqualified."

**MENTALLY PRACTICE.**
Imagine competition situations where you are the most concerned about messing up. Imagine the competition as a practice with friendly people watching who tell you, "It's okay when you lose your stirrup." Make them more and more hostile, and make your response to the problems faster and more professional.

Realize that it does not matter what they think. It's what you think that matters.

### VIVID AND REAL.

See the crowd and feel the tingles of adrenaline. Hear the loudspeaker, and the sensations of the heat and the noise. Imagine all the nervous butterflies you feel and realize that they are there to help you. Hear the things you say to yourself.

### BREAK INTO PIECES.

See the warm-up and the nerves and the thoughts you have as all separate variables. Make yourself more and less nervous, make the crowd larger and smaller, make them excited, make them cranky. Realize that your performance is the only part you can control, and picture how you will do that.

### PHYSICALLY PRACTICE.

Go to as many shows as possible. Watch others ride and realize that everyone messes up, even the best riders. Get important people whose opinions you value to watch you ride in practice. Put the pressure on yourself that way in the practice setting.

### DEFEAT IRRATIONAL THOUGHTS AND IMAGES DURING MENTAL AND PHYSICAL PRACTICE.

Give up the idea that perfectionism is the goal of a good competitor. You are a beginner and you are bound to mess up. Give up the idea that you need to impress people to be good.

### RECOGNIZE.

"I can see that holding on to this idea that I have to be perfect is stressing me out. I've got to think about riding to do well, not fear."

### STOP.

NO! NO! NO! STOP! BANG!

**DISPUTE.**

"I am demanding a level of perfection from myself that even the masters at this sport cannot attain. I am being an absolutist and demanding something that nobody could do . . . and that is crazy. I should be working on my performance, not on judging myself."

**REPLACE.**

"I have practiced mentally and physically and I may not be perfect . . . nobody is, but I'm going to go out there and use this performance to see how much I've improved. Sure I want to be great at this . . . but I'm expecting a bit much of myself at this stage of my training and I just need to leave myself alone and let myself ride."

## CASE FOUR

SITUATION.
Experienced rider who has fear of failing.

WHY DO THIS?
"This is a sport I've done for many years, and I've gotten quite good at it. It's something I hope to do for the rest of my life—I'm not going to quit. I just want to stop being so worried that all my practice won't pay off."

AM I AFRAID?
"Yes. I am afraid that I won't get to be as good as I wanted because I get too worried when I ride."

DO I KNOW WHY I AM AFRAID?
"I think so. If I am not good enough, if I don't uphold a certain standard I've set for myself, then I won't respect myself and maybe my peers won't respect me either."

IS THIS SOMETHING THAT I NEED TO DO?
"Yes, I like it and the rush I get from doing competitions. I just wish I wouldn't get so uptight about it."

WHAT ARE MY THOUGHTS AND IMAGES WHEN I'M FEARFUL?
"I just always see myself doing something stupid and messing that one thing up that seems to always keep me in third or fourth place. I know it is going to happen ahead of time—and it always happens."

MENTALLY PRACTICE.
Imagine that you are at a show and that you have gotten your customary one thing wrong. Figure out what it is that you did wrong and then go back and mentally ride the course again and correct it. Do that over and over with as many different scenarios as you can. Eventually begin riding the course *the first time as if*

*you had already corrected the problem.* Get comfortable with
doing it right the first time in your mind.

### VIVID AND REAL.

See all the details of the situation—all the aspects of the performance that generally bother you, and all the aspects that generally you get wrong. Picture the errors and the corrections as vividly
as possible. Be especially vivid and real when imagining doing it
right the first time.

### BREAK INTO PIECES.

See the mental drill as composed of two parts. In one part, concentrate on identifying the elements you feel you are likely to
mess up. In the second part, concentrate on doing correctly the
things you fear messing up.

### PHYSICALLY PRACTICE.

Take the things that you fear messing up and make them the
centerpiece of your practices. On purpose, begin in the middle of
your routine so that you are disoriented and need to figure out
where you should be. Master that. Build up all the pressure in
the world in your own mind over one particular skill. Pretend
everyone is watching you and work on doing it until you get it
right. Use competitions as practice also. Feel the tingles . . .
accept them as something good and go out there and take some
healthy risks.

### DEFEAT IRRATIONAL THOUGHTS AND IMAGES DURING
### MENTAL AND PHYSICAL PRACTICE.

"I think that I'm the only one out here who gets so nervous. I
am such a loser. All this practice for all these years and then I fall
apart on the day of competition and don't do as well as I'd like."

RECOGNIZE.

"That kind of thinking is definitely *not* going to help me win anything . . . or for that matter even have fun!"

STOP.

NO! NO! NO! STOP! BANG!

DISPUTE.

"What makes me so special that I'm the *only* one who always feels nervous. Everybody feels nervous when something big is happening. I'm not a loser just because I feel nervous and I mess up. *Everybody* messes up . . . even at the Olympics people mess up. I'm demanding that I not feel nerves and not mess up . . . that is like asking me not to be human."

REPLACE

"You know, all that tension and nervous feeling is good for me if I can learn to reinterpret it and use it to my best advantage. I've practiced quite a bit and I'm pretty good at what I do . . . maybe all that adrenaline is the advantage I should be *seeking*, not the disadvantage I should be *avoiding*. I think I'm going to use this stuff to help me win!"

## CASE FIVE

**SITUATION.**

Experienced rider with competition anxiety

**WHY DO THIS?**

"This is what I do. I cannot imagine not competing. Even though I feel sick before I ride, I really want to keep trying to do it."

**AM I AFRAID?**

"Yes. I don't like the way I feel before I compete. It frightens me."

**DO I KNOW WHY I AM AFRAID?**

"I think so. My identity and self-esteem are totally dependent on my continuing success as a competitive rider."

**IS THIS SOMETHING I NEED TO DO?**

"Yes. It is the reason I train and it is my way of living. I make a living doing this . . . and up until now it was a fun thing to do."

**WHAT ARE MY THOUGHTS AND IMAGES WHEN I'M FEARFUL?**

"I see that I have not made much of a name for myself, and I can see that I'm going to have to do something big to make that happen for me . . . and it doesn't seem to be happening. I see me making the okay living I'm making for the rest of my life and never really going to the big time."

**MENTALLY PRACTICE.**

Understand that no single moment defines a person. While each competition *is* important, thinking of them as very important to your *entire* future puts more pressure on you than any one competition needs to. What you need to concentrate on in practice is mentally accepting the adrenaline you feel as the fuel to help you be good. Examine your past and decide when you started to feel sick . . . probably when you started to think that you had to win every competition so you could make a name for yourself. Adrenaline is great stuff. It can help you win . . . as long as you take some time to enjoy the feeling.

### VIVID AND REAL.

Picture the exact situations when you feel sick and feel the adrenaline pounding in your veins. Compare how you feel now with how you would feel on a roller coaster. Which one is more fun? What's the difference? Likely the biggest difference is the way you decide to think about how you feel. Concentrate on enjoying and using the adrenaline to your best advantage.

### BREAK INTO PIECES

See the competition as composed of the actual event...and the way you feel about the event. Explore the reasons for your attitude and weigh how much benefit it has been. As far as we can see the extra pressure to perform is only going to worsen your performance. If you really want to give yourself a chance to be good, enjoy what you do and have a good time. The more you can enjoy it the longer you will practice and the more you like the adrenaline you feel. You need to concentrate on having the best experience for yourself—not on impressing anybody. Control yourself . . . because you cannot control others.

### PHYSICALLY PRACTICE.

Do what you used to do for practice. Go back to whatever fun routines you used to use when you did not take it all so seriously. The whole idea is to have some fun . . . and if you have fun you will practice more . . . feel less pressure . . . and have less fear and anxiety when you compete.

**DEFEAT IRRATIONAL THOUGHTS AND IMAGES DURING MENTAL AND PHYSICAL PRACTICE.**

"I must make it big here . . . this might be my last chance. I have to be great or I'll never make it."

**RECOGNIZE.**

"I can see that I'm pretty miserable right now, and that my performances are sliding because of the rotten time I am having. All the time I'm thinking terrible stuff about myself. It can't be helping."

**STOP.**

NO! NO! NO! STOP! BANG!

**DISPUTE.**

"I am not going to *make it* or *not make it* based on one jump, one ride, one day, one performance. That is not what this whole thing is about. I cannot control making it or not. I cannot control what others think of me. I can control my attitude and the absolutist thoughts I have about *having* to make it big and *demanding* perfect performances and people's attention."

**REPLACE.**

"I am the luckiest guy on the face of this planet. I get to make a decent living off of doing the thing that I love . . . *ride*. There are very few who can say that.. I'm lucky and I should enjoy the day to day because that is how people improve . . . day by day, not by *making it* or not."

## CASE SIX

SITUATION.

Fear of jumping.

**WHY DO THIS?**

Always wanted to jump. Started to ride because she watched other people jump and found it exciting. She is determined to overcome this fear so she can accomplish her goal.

**AM I AFRAID?**

"Yes," she admits to herself, "I go out to jump, watch others jump, and get inspired. The minute I realize that I will attempt to jump, I become nervous and afraid."

**DO I KNOW WHY I AM AFRAID?**

"No. It puzzles me. I am very attracted to the sport of jumping and these nervous fearful feelings are very unexpected. Perhaps my fear is the result of knowing all the things that can go wrong, such as losing control of the horse, getting injured, or failing. But these fears are rational, and my nervousness is becoming irrational and overtaking me. I need to regain control of my thoughts when preparing to jump."

**IS THIS SOMETHING I NEED TO DO?**

"This is something that was my goal from the beginning. I will not be satisfied if I do not attempt this goal."

**WHAT ARE MY THOUGHTS AND IMAGES WHEN I'M FEARFUL?**

"I see myself falling off of the horse during the jump. I am afraid that the horse will refuse the jump, and I won't be ready for it. I will fall on my head and get hurt, and others around me will know that I am a terrible rider. I don't feel safe. I don't feel comfortable."

## MENTALLY PRACTICE.

Get a mental picture of the horse you ride as it is jumping. Picture yourself in control and making a successful jump.

## VIVID AND REAL.

See all of the details. See the fence, see how you are holding your heels down, see your hands low. Imagine the approaching fence, and everything that you will see before, during, and after the jump.

## BREAK INTO PIECES.

See yourself in control as you ready yourself for the jump. Picture the horse and yourself as you approach a small fence. See yourself having a successful jump. Picture what you did to accomplish the task and then see yourself jump a larger fence successfully. Increase the size of the jump at each step.

## PHYSICALLY PRACTICE.

Start with a small jump and become comfortable with the skill. Continue until you become actually bored with the jump. You are then ready to increase the size. Think to yourself, "No jump is too big *or* too small for me. I must become so used to jumping a small fence that I am no longer afraid. If I continue this, I will be able to handle the larger ones in time."

## DEFEAT IRRATIONAL THOUGHTS AND IMAGES DURING MENTAL AND PHYSICAL PRACTICE.

"Everyone will laugh at me if I can't jump the larger fences. I am embarrassed to jump those tiny fences. It isn't exciting to me and I don't want to waste my time with it. I want to get to the exciting stuff!"

## RECOGNIZE.

"These negative thoughts are not going to help me jump. I started riding because I found the jumping exciting. I want to reach my goal."

**STOP.**

NO! NO! NO! STOP! BANG!

**DISPUTE.**

"I am demanding too much of myself too soon. I need to learn to walk before I can run. Every time I even think about jumping a larger fence or approach a larger fence, I am afraid. If I want to overcome my fear I must try with smaller jumps."

**REPLACE.**

"I have mentally and physically practiced jumping small jumps a million times. The more I jump, the better I feel. I am not as afraid when I approach a jump. I feel more comfortable and confident. If I have trouble or I feel afraid, I will adjust my expectations, practice more on the smaller jumps, until I can approach a larger jump with less anxiety."

## CASE SEVEN

SITUATION.

"I am scared to death of losing my place during my dressage test."

WHY DO THIS?

"I would never dream of quitting just because I cannot remember my tests . . . but it sure makes competitions uncomfortable for me."

AM I AFRAID?

"Well I guess I am afraid of looking like an idiot out there. I am also a little afraid of blowing my money on a test that I mess up like that."

DO I KNOW WHY I AM AFRAID?

"Yes. Lately I have become very forgetful about things. I have even forgotten my routine during practice sessions."

IS THIS SOMETHING THAT I NEED TO DO?

"Yes. Competing is the way I meet people, have fun, test myself and my horse, and see how far I've traveled in my training. I need to do it to stay happy."

WHAT ARE MY THOUGHTS AND IMAGES WHEN I'M FEARFUL?

"I think about all the training and the money that I'm wasting by making stupid mistakes. I think about how dumb I must look to all those folks who have more money and can afford to goof whenever they feel like it. I imagine myself as a clumsy-looking fool out there whenever I ride."

MENTALLY PRACTICE.

Ride the test a million times in your head and see yourself in every possible angle. Ride the test in your head as if you were actually riding, and then also watch yourself riding the test from as many different angles as possible. Do it over and over until you are sick of it.

### VIVID AND REAL.

Imagine the ring and the dust flying off of it on a hot day. Feel the horse's sweat soaking through your leather gloves and making a leathery smell. Put yourself on the horse. And then also put yourself in the stands and watch yourself from all different angles of the ring.

### BREAK INTO PIECES.

See each part of the test in chunks of "threes." Remember three sections as one piece and then another three sections as the next piece, and so on. When you memorize in "chunks," the first piece of the chunk will trigger the other pieces. When you start the first section of a chunk you will remember the rest of it as well.

### PHYSICALLY PRACTICE.

Ride the test . . . but not in order or your horse will learn to anticipate. You want him to listen, not anticipate. Practice the chunks out of order so that you will remember the components. Practice each unit of three.

### DEFEAT IRRATIONAL THOUGHTS AND IMAGES DURING MENTAL AND PHYSICAL PRACTICE.

"I *am* definitely going to mess this test up. I always do. I'm never going to get this right."

### RECOGNIZE.

"That kind of thinking is only putting more pressure on me."

### STOP.

NO! NO! NO! STOP! BANG!

DISPUTE.

"I can't rate myself as *always* no good and *never* going to get it based on a few mess ups! That's crazy. Look at all the good practice I've done so far. All I need to do is concentrate on the chunks of three that I've memorized and I'll be set. I may mess up ... but every time I'm going to get better. Everyone has a different challenge, and mine is remembering the test ... and if I practice well I *will*."

REPLACE.

"I'm going to mess up from time to time...and that is just the way it is going to be. But if I practice mentally and physically over and over, the chances of forgetting the test or getting lost in the middle of it are going to get really slim. I'm going to be really good at this one of these days, and all I need to do is keep practicing!"

## CASE EIGHT

**SITUATION.**

What to do if you actually lose your place during a routine.

**WHY DO THIS?**

"Keep going. It would be more defeating to stop in the middle and quit."

**AM I AFRAID?**

"Yes! I'm afraid that everyone is watching me and feeling bad for me and thinking I'm so stupid. They are all thinking, 'I'm glad I'm not her!' "

**DO I KNOW WHY I AM AFRAID?**

"Yes. I'm afraid I might have to admit that I'm not perfect. I don't want to look in the mirror and see a mere mortal."

**IS THIS SOMETHING I NEED TO DO?**

"Yes. I need to face this fear head-on and gain acceptance of the fact that mistakes can happen, that I am human."

**WHAT ARE MY THOUGHTS AND IMAGES WHEN I AM FEARFUL?**

"I just freeze and think, 'My God what am I going to do!' and then I get red in the face and quit."

**MENTALLY PRACTICE.**

Mentally practice doing something instead of nothing when you are lost on the course. Make a move . . . the best guess you have of the next logical step of the test. There is *absolutely* no harm in doing the next thing you *think* is next. You'd be surprised how many times you pick the right thing next. Remember everything in chunks of three and overmemorize by going over the test mentally as many times as you can. Concentrate on the memorization of the chunks. If you do this long enough...the first piece of the chunk of three elements will cue the next ones and you will have a well-ingrained memory of the skills that will be nearly automatic. That means that you will often be able to "guess" where you should go next, and—if you relax and let yourself—your mind will pick the right direction.

### VIVID AND REAL.

See the test and memorize it as best you can using the mental chunking method. See every detail. Note where each chunk starts and each one ends. Picture the chunks as landmarks in the ring. Those landmarks will help you if you get lost.

### BREAK INTO PIECES.

The chunks are the pieces that you need to work on.

### PHYSICALLY PRACTICE.

Practice pieces of the test separate from each other. Imagine the parts before it and the parts after it to help you memorize the test. Don't practice the whole test all together with your horse because he will begin to anticipate the moves and will be less responsive in the ring.

### DEFEAT IRRATIONAL THOUGHTS AND IMAGES DURING MENTAL AND PHYSICAL PRACTICE.

"In practice and in actual competition, I feel like I'm just inches away from losing my train of thought, of losing my place in the test all the time. I'm so scared that I will lose my place and then be embarrassed again that it makes me freeze in place when I do."

### RECOGNIZE.

"This is not a helpful attitude to take toward messing up. It makes me mess up when I feel that way. I know it would be better to do *anything* than to freeze and do nothing."

### STOP.

NO! NO! NO! STOP! BANG!

**DISPUTE.**

"This is a demand for perfection and for everyone to like me and think I'm good at this sport. What I really need to remember is that I need to trust myself, and whatever my brain tells me is the right way to go is likely to be correct if I've practiced well. Even when I mess up from time to time I know that there are plenty of others out there who mess up too. I'm not the only one. The only reason people feel bad for me is that they are afraid of getting lost too. All I need to do is keep going."

**REPLACE.**

"Whenever I feel like freezing and stopping, I'm just going to keep going . . . wherever my brain says is probably the right way. If I'm wrong who cares . . . I was going to be wrong anyhow. If I'm right, Great! I will know that I did a great job memorizing the test, and that I really trusted myself. If I mess up then that is *simply a sign that I'm human*, nothing worse.

## CASE NINE

SITUATION.

Fear of going off pattern in a western pleasure class competition.

WHY DO THIS?

"I am a successful competitor and am not ready to quit competing."

AM I AFRAID?

"Yes. I don't want to mess up, especially if I have a chance to do well. I fear making the stupid mistakes and messing the whole thing up."

DO I KNOW WHY I AM AFRAID?

"I feel like my memory is slipping. I am losing my place more frequently."

IS THIS SOMETHING THAT I NEED TO DO?

"Yes. I want to compete. I've always enjoyed doing it. I feel that I am not as sharp as I used to be. I want to keep trying, to see if I can pull out of this slump."

WHAT ARE MY THOUGHTS AND IMAGES WHEN I'M FEARFUL?

"I imagine my enjoyment of riding slipping away because I might not get the routines right. I'm afraid that it might suck the joy out the sport if I'm always messing up. I guess I can see my outlet of fun slipping away."

MENTALLY PRACTICE.

Spend some time thinking about the sections of the routine. Think about the sections over and over. Have each section composed of only two or three pieces and go over those pieces over and over. Mentally ride the routine as many times as you can paying special attention when each "chunk" starts and when each chunk ends.

VIVID AND REAL.

See all the parts of the class a clearly as you can. Feel the horse under you, see the ring, smell the dust and the leather. Imagine riding correctly over and over again.

BREAK INTO PIECES.

Concentrate on the chunks. Especially think about the way the chunks fit into the whole. Concentrate on the chunks that have the toughest parts.

PHYSICALLY PRACTICE.

Repeatedly practice each of the subsection "chunks" as individual pieces (but not all together as your horse may grow to anticipate . . . and you want him to listen, not to anticipate. Practice until each chunk is overlearned. Then mentally stick all the chunks together for practice.

DEFEAT IRRATIONAL THOUGHTS AND IMAGES DURING MENTAL AND PHYSICAL PRACTICE.

"I'm *never* going to be able to enjoy this sport again, because I am *always* going to be afraid of forgetting where I am.

RECOGNIZE.

"I can see that these thoughts cause me to feel upset and feel disturbed and that it might make me want to stop competing. What I really need to do is keep this sport fun for me."

STOP.

NO! NO! NO! STOP! BANG!

DISPUTE.

"I will not let these thoughts ruin my fun. I can see that I'm trying to rate myself on just a couple of experiences as *never* being able to enjoy again, and *always* having problems remembering the routine. I cannot demand that I always remember. Forgetting happens. I would *prefer* to get this right and not mess up . . . but everyone does. Just because I want this to be fun does not mean it will *always be fun*. Some days will be better than others.

**REPLACE.**

"I'm going to go out there and do the things I've practiced . . . and if I mess up, so be it. Everyone messes up. I'll shake it off and get on to the next one. I'm trying to *demand* that I have a good time. I should just go out there and enjoy and let the good times happen.

## CASE TEN

**SITUATION.**
What to do if you actually go off pattern.

**WHY DO THIS?**
"Because I enjoy the competitions and the camaraderie."

**AM I AFRAID?**
"Yes. I'm afraid that my friends won't like me as much because they can see that I'm not as good of a rider as they thought."

**IS THIS SOMETHING THAT I NEED TO DO?**
"Well it certainly is not that dangerous . . . and it is a lot of fun, plus I like the social end of the shows too. Yes, I think of it as something that I need to do."

**WHAT ARE MY THOUGHTS AND IMAGES WHEN I'M FEARFUL.**
"I think about the way everyone sees me from outside the ring. I think they see me as no good."

**MENTALLY PRACTICE.**
Work on thinking of yourself and simply reacting. Memorize the heck out of the test by remembering it as chunks of two or three moves per section, but then when you get out to the ring let yourself go. Practice the routine in your mind as many times as you can stand, and particularly concentrate on the chunks of two to three moves apiece. Work on memorizing the test, and then on becoming comfortable with letting it all go when you ride. Be able to be a little impulsive out there. If you cannot remember where you need to go, take your best guess and do it. Doing anything is better than nothing in this case . . . even if you are wrong.

**VIVID AND REAL.**

Picture all of the people around the ring and the way you feel when you go in. Mentally picture where each chunk of information begins and ends. Mentally practice it with as crisp an image as possible. If you get stuck on the visualization, do *anything*. Go wherever makes the most sense. You will find that you will be on target more times than not.

**BREAK INTO PIECES.**

Concentrate on the chunks of the routine. Work on memorizing the chunks and mentally riding them and then mentally putting them all together. Realize that if you memorize the chunks well, they will be lodged firmly in you brain and then you can trust that your practice will show up during competition . . . even when you get stuck!

**PHYSICALLY PRACTICE.**

Ride the pieces of the performance over and over, but not together (so that your horse will not begin to "jump the gun," and anticipate). Practice the chunks over and over so that by triggering the first element of the chunk the next ones immediately come to mind.

**DEFEAT IRRATIONAL THOUGHTS AND IMAGES DURING MENTAL AND PHYSICAL PRACTICE.**

"If I mess up my friends will see that I'm not that good and that would be *terrible*. I would hate it if I goofed; then I would not be able to go on. I'd be too embarrassed."

**RECOGNIZE.**

"I can see that my thoughts are getting in my way and might cause me to freeze. I've got to do my best to feel good, and dwelling on negatives sure won't help me!"

**STOP.**

NO! NO! NO! STOP BANG!

DISPUTE.

"If my friends really like me then they are still going to like me when I mess up. There are some things I *can* control, like my thoughts and my actions. I'm thinking crazy if I'm trying to control what others think of me. I'm also thinking crazy when I feel like it is the worst thing in the world when I mess up. The best thing for me to do is to keep going and try things *even if I am wrong*."

REPLACE.

"I am going to go out there and ride my best and think my best thoughts and trust the instincts that I have honed through many mental run-throughs in practice and many times of practicing the pieces in practice. I'm going to do my best because that is all I can do . . . and let the chips fall where they may. I am *not* perfect, and I *will* mess up and that is a given. What I should concentrate on are the things I *can* do . . . which are practice and trust. If I get hung up in the middle of the routine, I'm just going to take my best guess and keep going."

## CASE ELEVEN

**SITUATION.**

Unsure of a horse—fear of losing control of a horse.

**WHY DO THIS?**

She enjoys riding, especially on trails.

**AM I AFRAID?**

"Yes. I am afraid that I will lose control of the horse and will not be able to handle him."

**DO I KNOW WHY I AM AFRAID?**

"It really disturbs me to the core of my being when a horse leaves my control during exercises. I can sense it right away and it leaves me cold. I think perhaps the 'control issue' is a significant one for me. But I understand that it is critical to be in charge of your mount when riding."

**IS THIS SOMETHING THAT I NEED TO DO?**

"In order to enjoy riding, I must conquer the control issue in a positive way. Riding used to be fun, before I realized all of the things that could go wrong. I want it to become fun for me again. And I want to be in control for the majority of the time."

**WHAT ARE MY THOUGHTS AND IMAGES WHEN I'M FEARFUL?**

"I see the horse running off with me. I see myself falling off and getting hurt because I can't control the horse. I don't feel safe or in control. I think to myself, 'I'm not having fun.'"

**MENTALLY PRACTICE.**

Begin by picturing the horse you ride and the situations where you feel most fearful. For example, the horse is startled by something and runs off with you.

VIVID AND REAL.

Picture everything around you. Hear the startling sound and picture you and your horse's reaction to it.

BREAK INTO PIECES.

Picture yourself with your heels down and ready for anything. See the horse startled and feel yourself respond to it. See that your heels are down and that you can handle it. Picture yourself remaining calm as the horse begins to run off with you. See yourself successfully gaining control.

PHYSICALLY PRACTICE.

Practice riding defensively, keeping your heels down and being ready for anything. Practice being aware of anything that might startle the horse.

DEFEAT IRRATIONAL THOUGHTS AND IMAGES DURING MENTAL AND PHYSICAL PRACTICE.

"I will not be able to handle this horse if something happens. I am never in control . . . the horse is. I might as well stay by the barn, in the ring, where unpredictable things rarely happen."

RECOGNIZE.

"I want to enjoy riding. I must realize that I can work on becoming less fearful. These negative thoughts will prevent me from getting enjoyment out of the sport."

STOP.

NO! NO! NO! STOP! BANG!

DISPUTE.

"I am demanding absolute safety from my riding experience and absolute perfection in how I respond to unpredictable situations. *Everyone* gets hurt. I need to realize that I can prevent some injuries by being prepared for the unpredictable and aware of possible problems. I need to concentrate on smart riding, and *not* on my fears!"

**REPLACE.**

"I have learned how to ride safely and have mentally and physically practiced how to prevent possible injuries. I have learned to become aware of my surroundings to better predict possible problems. I am ready to handle anything that happens. If I become injured, I know that I did all that was possible and that I can deal with that."

## CASE TWELVE

SITUATION.
History of unproductive practice sessions—uncertainty of horse.

WHY DO THIS?
"I want to improve so that I can be a competitive rider."

AM I AFRAID?
"I am afraid that I will not be able to succeed and that I don't work well with my horse."

DO I KNOW WHY I AM AFRAID?
"It has been suggested to me by someone whose opinion I value that I shouldn't compete on this horse (we have several upcoming shows) until we work out our communication problems."

IS THIS SOMETHING THAT I NEED TO DO?
"In order to compete, I must have successful practices. My reason for riding is to compete."

WHAT ARE MY THOUGHTS AND IMAGES WHEN I'M FEARFUL?
"I feel like a failure after practice. I am afraid that I will not be able to compete. My horse does not respond to me. I am a terrible rider who can't even control her own horse. I will never be successful. I should just give up now."

MENTALLY PRACTICE.
Picture you and your horse having a successful, productive practice. See that your horse is responding well to you and that you have accomplished most of the goals you set for that day.

VIVID AND REAL.
Picture all of the details of the practice. See how you ride—how you hold your hands, how straight your back is, and how your heels are down.

### BREAK INTO PIECES.

Set small goals for each practice. Keep the goals reasonable. Congratulate yourself for accomplishing the goals you met, knowing that you can succeed at the other goals during your next practice. Increase the difficulty of the goals you set only after you have experienced some success. Separate parts of the practice that went well from parts that did not go well. Realize that if all of the parts that didn't go well are due to your horse, you might have to consider that the horse is the problem. Determine if you should keep the horse.

### PHYSICALLY PRACTICE.

"I have set only a few small goals for practice today. I will work on each goal for as long as I need to. If I don't get to them all today, there is always tomorrow."

### DEFEAT IRRATIONAL THOUGHTS AND IMAGES DURING MENTAL AND PHYSICAL PRACTICE.

"I can't even meet these tiny goals that I have set for myself. I will never be any good. I will never be able to compete. Even my horse can tell I'm not any good."

### RECOGNIZE.

"I really want to compete. It is what I have always wanted to do. Thinking that I am no good is not going to help me improve."

### STOP.

NO! NO! NO! STOP! BANG!

### DISPUTE.

"I am demanding too much of myself too soon. I must set small goals for myself, experience success, and then move on to more difficult goals."

—or—

"I must realize that sometimes the horse is the problem. It isn't

because I am doing things wrong that the horse is not responding to me. The horse is just not right for me. I can't change him,
so why try? I should get another horse."

**REPLACE.**

"I have set some good, reasonable goals. I can achieve them and
move on to bigger and better things, but at a pace that suits me.
I will get to where I want to go, I just have to learn to take it
one step at a time."

## CASE THIRTEEN

**SITUATION.**

Fear of the unexpected on a trail ride.

**WHY DO THIS?**

I used to enjoy spending time trail-riding with friends. It used to be my favorite way to spend time.

**AM I AFRAID?**

"I am afraid every time I go out. So many unexpected things could happen. The horse could become startled and I am afraid I couldn't handle it."

**DO I KNOW WHY I AM AFRAID?**

"Several months ago a friend's young daughter had a terrible accident after her horse was startled by something on a trail ride far from the barn. The whole thing was so unexpected: Everyone was riding on their own horses; the horses all seemed to be of good dispositions that day; the weather was beautiful; and suddenly, everything went wrong. The girl's injuries were severe and her situation was worsened by her distance from the farm and the time it took to get her to emergency medical help."

**IS THIS SOMETHING THAT I NEED TO DO?**

"I am grieving for the loss of my favorite activity, a relaxing trail ride. It's as if I have been wounded psychologically and want to become healthy again. Yes, I definitely need to ride again, to conquer this fear, in order to be healed."

**WHAT ARE MY THOUGHTS AND IMAGES WHEN I'M FEARFUL?**

"I am afraid that the horse will be startled and I will not be able to control him. I am afraid that we will fall and I will get hurt. I am afraid that I will be too far from home to get help."

**MENTALLY PRACTICE.**

Begin by imaging your horse and the situations that may occur. Picture yourself remaining in control and staying calm.

**VIVID AND REAL.**

Picture your surroundings—the trees, the fences, the other horses and riders with you. See how you keep your heels down and keep control of the horse as something unexpected happens.

**BREAK INTO PIECES.**

Picture yourself with your heels down and ready for anything. See the horse startled and feel yourself respond to it. See that your heels are down and that you can handle it. Picture yourself remaining calm as the horse reacts to the unexpected. See yourself successfully gaining control.

**PHYSICALLY PRACTICE.**

Learn how to stay alert on the trail, while still enjoying yourself. Become confident in your preparedness. Practice how to ride so that you will be ready for anything—keeping your heels down and your eyes open.

**DEFEAT IRRATIONAL THOUGHTS AND IMAGES DURING MENTAL AND PHYSICAL PRACTICE.**

"I will not be able to handle the horse if something happens. I will fall off and become hurt. The horse is so much stronger than I, I will never be in control."

**RECOGNIZE.**

"I love riding the trail with my friends. I know that people do get hurt, but that I must overcome my fears in order to enjoy what I love."

**STOP.**

NO! NO! NO! STOP! BANG!

**DISPUTE.**

"I am demanding that I be ready for everything and that I control everything. No one can predict what is going to happen and no one is totally safe. I need to focus on how to ride as safely as I can and *not* on my fears."

**REPLACE.**

"I have practiced mentally and physically for any possibility. I am ready for practically anything, but know that I can't control what might happen on the trail. I know that I might get hurt, but I can increase my safety by riding smart. I will enjoy riding knowing that I am prepared as much as anyone can be. I will carry a cellular telephone when I ride out away from the barn in order to keep in touch."

## CASE FOURTEEN

**SITUATION.**

Approaching a terrifying fence on a trail ride.

**WHY DO THIS?**

"I have always wanted to be a competitive steeplechase jockey. I must face the fear, or I won't be able to compete."

—or—

"I don't need to do this in order to get what I want out of riding, but others expect me to do it."

**AM I AFRAID?**

"I am afraid that I won't be able to race competitively and that others will view me as a failure."

—or—

"I am afraid that if I choose not to do this, others will view me as a failure."

**DO I KNOW WHY I AM AFRAID?**

"Yes. I expect much from myself and believe that others expect the same from me. I am very unnerved by obstacles to my success, as this fence might be. I don't want to disappoint myself and everybody else."

**IS THIS SOMETHING THAT I NEED TO DO?**

"In order to compete, I must overcome my fears. I began to ride because I wanted to compete. It has always been my dream."

—or—

"I don't really need to do this. If I were out on the trail alone, I would either turn around, ride around the fence, or get off the horse and lead him around. If others were around, I would be embarrassed. But, I don't *need* to do this to get what I want out of riding."

**WHAT ARE MY THOUGHTS AND IMAGES WHEN I'M FEARFUL?**

"I see the horse refusing the fence and me falling and getting hurt. I see myself falling off the horse during the jump and injuring myself. I also feel that I am not competent enough to handle such a large fence. I am not a good enough rider and I am never going to be able to ride competitively."

—or—

"I feel embarrassed that I can't do it. I feel as if I am a failure and that others would see me that way if I choose not to jump it."

**MENTALLY PRACTICE.**

Picture the horse jumping the fence while you are in total control.

—or—

Picture the fence and decide whether it is more than you can handle.

**VIVID AND REAL.**

See the fence as you are approaching. Feel the horse jumping it as you guide him over it successfully.

—or—

Picture the trail and the fence. See everything around you, including your different options.

**BREAK INTO PIECES.**

See the fence, and approach it in stages. Feel yourself getting prepared for the jump. Feel your horse getting ready to jump and responding to you. See yourself going over the jump successfully.

—or—

See the fence. Compare it to other fences you have jumped successfully. Determine if it is too big for you to handle. Determine what your options are—go around, turn back, or dismount.

## PHYSICALLY PRACTICE.

Practice jumping over different sized fences. Start with small ones you can handle. After experiencing many successes, increase the size of the fence. Continue to do so until you feel comfortable jumping large fences.

—or—

There is no need to physically practice fences that are too big for you! Try to avoid them. If you cannot, exercise the different options you may have—turn back, go around it, or stop your horse.

## DEFEAT IRRATIONAL THOUGHTS AND IMAGES DURING MENTAL AND PHYSICAL PRACTICE.

"I will never be able to do this. I am too afraid of the large fences. I panic when I see them. I will never be able to reach my dream."

—or—

"If I don't jump this fence, people will laugh at me."

## RECOGNIZE.

"My dream is to ride competitively. In order to do so, I must overcome these fears. Thinking that I can't do it will not help me to reach my dreams."

—or—

"I don't really need to do this to get what I want out of riding. Thinking about what others might think of me will not help me make the right decision."

## STOP.

NO! NO! NO! STOP! BANG!

## DISPUTE.

"I am demanding too much of myself. I need to realize that no one starts out jumping the very large fences. Everyone has to start somewhere."

—or—

"I shouldn't care what other people think. I am doing this because I enjoy it. Why try to do something I don't need to do or don't want to do?"

**REPLACE.**

"I have practiced mentally and physically and I am ready to face a large jump. I have built up my skills over time, and know that I can do it."

—or—

"I do not need to prove anything to anyone. I don't need to jump the fence. I have the intelligence to make a smart decision. I don't need to risk injury."

## CASE FIFTEEN

**SITUATION.**
What to do if you lose a stirrup.

**WHY DO THIS?**
Losing and regaining stirrups is a part of the game. It is as much a part of riding as horses are.

**AM I AFRAID?**
"Yes! That would be horrible. I'd probably die!"

**DO I KNOW WHY I AM AFRAID?**
"For starters, I have never before lost a stirrup. I realize it has got to happen sometime. I fear the unknown."

**IS THIS SOMETHING I NEED TO DO?**
"Well since I love to ride, and I'm scared to death of losing my stirrups, I think I have a problem. I really want to keep going with the riding, but it is a rotten feeling. I know everybody loses their stirrup from time to time but I'm still scared!"

**WHAT ARE MY THOUGHTS AND IMAGES WHEN I AM FEARFUL?**
"I pretty much see my life passing before my eyes. I picture myself falling on my head and getting really hurt."

**MENTALLY PRACTICE.**
Work on a vision of when you feel the most confident when you are riding. Mentally work on the accuracy of that image; make it as real as possible. From that point all the mental exercise will start.

**VIVID AND REAL.**
Imagine that you are riding at your most confident moment and picture how that feels and looks. Place yourself in your favorite environment . . . maybe a ring or even in the stall.

**BREAK INTO PIECES.**

Break the loss of the stirrup into sections. Begin with the most confident moment and, maintaining your level of confidence, mentally slide your toe little by little out of the stirrup. Do that until you can get it out and put it back at the halt, and then the walk and so on. Mentally practice this and the strategies you would use to get the stirrup back. Imagine how you would hold the reins and how you would sit . . . think about all the elements. Think about it with a lead or on the lunge . . . and then gradually without either.

**PHYSICALLY PRACTICE.**

As a part of your physical practice try dropping your feet out of the stirrups at the halt and then fishing around for them without your hands to get them back. Have somebody hold the horse if necessary. Do this over and over. Next, try at the walk and so on after that. In the beginning you can start on a lead or on the lunge or on your own. Gradually try for greater and greater independence in your physical practice.

**DEFEAT IRRATIONAL THOUGHTS AND IMAGES DURING MENTAL AND PHYSICAL PRACTICE.**

"If I lose my stirrups I'm going to get killed. It is terrible. It is the worst thing in the world. I know I'll definitely get hurt badly."

**RECOGNIZE.**

"I can see that adding all this pressure on top of the fact that it is a tough task to get your stirrup back when you lose it could lead to an even worse time. I think that the best thing for me to think about when it is time to get my stirrup back is how to get my stirrup back . . . not on how I'm going to get squashed."

**STOP.**

NO! NO! NO! STOP! BANG!

**DISPUTE.**

" I may get hurt if I fall, but I probably won't get killed. I probably won't even get hurt that badly. In fact . . . if I can get my stirrup back I won't fall at all and so that is what is the most sensible thing for me to concentrate on. I am demanding too much from the whole riding experience. I know that it would be nice for everything to be easy and safe . . . but it isn't. I can make things safer for myself though if I learn some basic things, like how to get my stirrup back when I lose it."

**REPLACE.**

"I think that, if I hold onto the main and lean flat on the horse's neck, I can stay steady and not fall. Then I can poke around with my toes until I find the stirrups. Then I'll be all right."

## CASE SIXTEEN

**SITUATION.**

Your horse becomes excitable just before you enter the ring.

**WHY DO THIS?**

"Because this is a talented horse who has some problems. I'm a good rider, and I may be able to deal with this. I want to give this horse a chance before I give up on him."

**AM I AFRAID?**

"Yes. I'm a bit nervous because this horse tests me to the edge of my abilities. I'm not sure if I can deal with it . . . but it's still worth the chance for me."

**DO I KNOW WHY I AM AFRAID?**

"I don't trust myself to handle this situation appropriately. I have the tendency to react badly to this type of situation, causing my horse to act up even more."

**IS THIS SOMETHING I NEED TO DO?**

"Yes. I need to give the horse a try and I need to see if I can handle it. It is an important stage of growth in my career."

**WHAT ARE MY THOUGHTS AND IMAGES WHEN I'M FEARFUL?**

"I think about getting hurt badly, or the horse really flipping out during the class and maybe hurting someone else too."

**MENTALLY PRACTICE.**

At this level of riding, and with this type of horse, the best thing is to keep relaxed and ready. Concentrate in your imagery not on particular events, but just of a relaxed snug feel on the horse.

**VIVID AND REAL.**

Mentally concentrate on basics. The basics of your position and the basics of the horse's temperament. What are his usual routines? Prepare your ride mentally so that you have a little tighter rein on the side he might wheel away from. If he rears, be ready to duck you face to the side and grab neck. If he plunges be ready to lean back. If he stops or refuses, or is prone to sudden moves, imagine riding with long stirrups . . . relaxed and seated back on the saddle with legs forward just the slightest in a defensive posture.

## BREAK INTO PIECES

Organize the horse's quirks into categories and mentally rehearse general routines. Imagine what to do for a sudden move, and what to do if he feels like he'll buck. Imagine feeling relaxed and ready, and simply responding.

## PHYSICALLY PRACTICE.

Ride the horse as much as possible in a controlled home environment. Test the horse out in as many situations as possible at home so you can prepare for competition.

## DEFEAT IRRATIONAL THOUGHTS AND IMAGES DURING MENTAL AND PHYSICAL PRACTICE.

"This horse might just finish me off. It could really hurt me. I don't know why I'm doing this."

## RECOGNIZE.

"For somebody who has decided to take this talented horse and see if I can go far with him . . . I sure have a pretty bad attitude. Not a single one of those thoughts is helping me ride this horse. I already know that this is important to me so I'm not going to quit. I might as well keep my head in the game and do this thing the right way."

## STOP.

NO! NO! NO! STOP! BANG!

DISPUTE.

"Yes this horse could hurt me. I knew that going into this. I'm taking a calculated risk. I think I can handle this horse. Even if I can't . . . I am a good enough rider that I should be fine even if he really flips out. In fact, I think that I will have my answer that he is not suitable if he flips out badly enough . . . and then I will not have to worry about him. I will have to trust my instincts and realize that I might get hurt and that is the risk I chose when I took on this horse."

REPLACE.

"I'm going to try this horse and put up with anything he throws my way—even if it is frightening—because I think it is important for me. I know I'm taking a risk and I'm willing to deal with it. I trust my instincts enough to know when I should throw in the towel."

## CASE SEVENTEEN

**SITUATION.**

You are not comfortable riding a friend's horse.

**WHY DO THIS?**

"I don't want to hurt my friend's feelings. I also don't want to miss out on the chance to spend time with my friend. I only feel comfortable riding my own horse, and this limits what I can do. In order to be able to enjoy riding, I must learn to become more comfortable with horses other than my own."

**AM I AFRAID?**

"Yes, I am afraid that my friend will make fun of me or be mad at me. I am also afraid that I will hurt myself because I am not used to her horse."

**DO I KNOW WHY I AM AFRAID?**

"Yes. I am not confident enough in this friendship or in my own opinions to be frank with my friend about my feelings toward her horse, which are a result of my own limitations as a rider."

**IS THIS SOMETHING THAT I NEED TO DO?**

If you are uncomfortable riding your friend's horse for certain reasons (others have been hurt riding him, for example), go with your instinct. Do not ride him if you believe you can't control him and you have a reasonable chance of getting hurt. If, however, you are afraid to ride because you have only ridden your own horse(s), you need to determine if you want to be able to ride a strange horse. If there is no real risk to your safety, you should try to ride.

**WHAT ARE MY THOUGHTS AND IMAGES WHEN I'M FEARFUL?**

"I am not used to this horse. I have only ridden my own. He knows me and I know him. I know what to expect. I don't know what to expect with this horse. I have no idea what his personality is and how he will react to me. My friend told me about him, but how do I know he won't react to me differently?"

**MENTALLY PRACTICE.**

Picture yourself on this unfamiliar horse. Feel yourself adjusting to his personality. Picture yourself being flexible as you get to know him and he gets to know you.

**VIVID AND REAL.**

See the color of the horse and feel how he responds well to you. Feel how he is different from your horse, and adjust accordingly.

**BREAK INTO PIECES.**

Approach the horse slowly. Get to know him as you tack him up. Begin to establish a relationship with him on the ground, before you mount. When you begin to ride, start slowly. Start with things that you are very comfortable with. If you become uncomfortable or afraid, stop what you are doing and try something easier. Get to know the horse, over time, if possible. Do not over-challenge yourself. Take it easy, and enjoy every step of the way.

**PHYSICALLY PRACTICE.**

"I have now tacked him up and am ready to mount. I will begin slowly so that I remain comfortable. I can handle walking around the ring easily. I can accomplish this without any fears. I will then move on to things that are more difficult, but only after I have given myself enough time to become comfortable with the horse and the task. I want to become very bored with what I am doing. If I become bored, I know that I have conquered the fear and that I am ready for the next task."

## DEFEAT IRRATIONAL THOUGHTS AND IMAGES DURING MENTAL AND PHYSICAL PRACTICE.

"There is no way I can ride a horse that isn't my own. I have had years of experience with my horse. It takes too much time to build a relationship with a different horse. If I ride my friend's horse, I won't have control. He won't understand me and I won't understand him. I probably will fall off and get hurt. I might as well not even try."

### RECOGNIZE.

"I want to be able to ride with other people. I can't bring my horse everywhere. If I keep thinking I can't do it, I'll be riding alone for the rest of my life."

### STOP.

NO! NO! NO! STOP! BANG!

### DISPUTE.

"I am demanding perfection from myself and all horses. I want the perfect ride with a horse that knows me so well, I don't have to do any work. I need to realize that I can still have a good and safe ride with an unfamiliar horse. No ride will be perfect and not every relationship with every horse I ride is going to be built over a lifetime."

### REPLACE.

"I am prepared to take it one step at a time. I have mentally and physically practiced accomplishing small goals, and building from them. I know that I can't always have the perfect ride and that I can't expect perfection from an unfamiliar horse. I know that I need to be realistic, and that I can become comfortable with my friend's horse by having realistic goals.

## CASE EIGHTEEN

**SITUATION.**

Your horse is not with the program during a competition.

**WHY DO THIS?**

"Because I love to ride."

**AM I AFRAID?**

"Mildly. My horse is just out to lunch and it bugs me."

**DO I KNOW WHY I AM AFRAID?**

"I prefer the status quo. When my horse behaves differently it throws me off mentally and physically. It is important for me to always be in control of every situation."

**IS THIS SOMETHING THAT I NEED TO DO?**

"Yes. I need to ride because it is something that gives me great joy in life . . . even if my horse is not doing so well today."

**WHAT ARE MY THOUGHTS AND IMAGES WHEN I'M FEARFUL?**

"I'm mildly fearful about what is going to happen next, since things aren't going as I had planned, and I'm disappointed in my horse's lack of concentration. I wonder if my horse has any clue what he is doing."

**MENTALLY PRACTICE.**

Be ready to compensate for your horse when he is not on the ball. Envision the problem, and consider ways to help him out on the ride.

**VIVID AND REAL.**

Make the images of the circumstances as clear as possible.

**BREAK INTO PIECES.**

Imagine the skills you could use to activate your horse, and also to help him with the task at hand.

**PHYSICALLY PRACTICE.**

Use practice situations when your horse is "dragging" to try out different techniques to get his attention. Experiment with different aids and different styles.

**DEFEAT IRRATIONAL THOUGHTS AND IMAGES DURING MENTAL AND PHYSICAL PRACTICE.**

"My horse is so out to lunch that he'll never be able to get around this course. I can't believe what a loser of a horse I have."

**RECOGNIZE.**

"I would do a whole lot better trying to figure out a way to get my horse's attention rather than dwelling on his inadequacies."

**STOP.**

NO! NO! NO! STOP! BANG!

**DISPUTE.**

"You know this is just a horse. It think I might be asking a bit for an animal to be *exactly* what I want, especially since *people* cannot even be perfect."

**REPLACE.**

"I have a pretty nice horse who has some mental lapses from time to time. I can deal with that way better than one who might try to hurt me. I can deal with his failings if he can deal with mine."

# PHOTOGRAPHY CREDITS

- Page 18: Carol Lavell in the Barcelona Olympics. John Strassburger Photo/Courtesy of *The Chronicle of the Horse*

- Page 31: Bruce Davidson on Heyday. Tricia Booker Photo/Courtesy of *The Chronicle of the Horse*

- Page 35: Leslie Webb concentrating on the Pan Am silver medal. Tricia Booker Photo/Courtesy of *The Chronicle of the Horse*

- Page 38: Martha Josey and friend. Courtesy of Josey Enterprises, Inc.

- Page 41: Jeff Teter and Elberton Fling at Shenandoah (VA.). John De Michele Photo/Courtesy of *The Chronicle of the Horse*

- Page 45: Rodney Jenkins on Czar. John Strassburger Photo/Courtesy of *The Chronicle of the Horse*

- Page 49: Valerie Kanavy. Tricia Booker Photo/Courtesy of *The Chronicle of the Horse*

- Page 54: Greg Ryan on Crimson Tales. Robert Banner Photo/Courtesy of *The Chronicle of the Horse*

- Page 71: Bruce Davidson with Heyday (left) and Eagle Lion. John Strassburger Photo/Courtesy of *The Chronicle of the Horse*

- Page 97: Trans Am A Flirt and Bruce Davidson. John Strassburger Photo/Courtesy of *The Chronicle of the Horse*

- Page 102: Valerie Kanavy and Pieraz "cash." Tricia Booker Photo/Courtesy of *The Chronicle of the Horse*

- Page 107: Leslie Webb on Hannibal, Tricia Booker Photo/Courtesy of *The Chronicle of the Horse*

# ABOUT THE AUTHORS

Theresa J. Jordan, Ph.D., is a professional psychologist and faculty member of New York University. Dr. Jordan studied Rational Emotive Behavior Therapy with the theory's founder, Dr. Albert Ellis, at the Institute for REBT in New York City. Dr. Jordan rides, trains, and shows Icelandic horses and is a member of the U.S. Icelandic Demonstration Team.

Peter E. De Michele, M.Ed., is a doctoral candidate in sports psychology at the University of Virginia. Mr. De Michele is a professional steeplechase jockey, a certified U.S. Pony Club Instructor, and a life-long award-winning rider. He writes a regular and popular column on sports psychology for *The Chronicle of the Horse*.